MILES AND MOMENTS

A Voyage to Exquisite Cuisine, Culture and Commerce

MANYA BHATIA

STARDOM BOOKS

www.StardomBooks.com

STARDOM BOOKS
A Division of Stardom Publishing
and infoYOGIS Technologies.
105-501 Silverside Road
Wilmington, DE 19809

Copyright © 2022 by Manya Bhatia

This book is copyright under the Berne Convention.
No reproduction without permission.
All rights reserved.

The right of Manya Bhatia to be identified as the author
of this work has been asserted by her in accordance with
sections 77 and 78 of the Copyright, Designs and Patents
Act, 1988.

FIRST EDITION JULY 2022

STARDOM BOOKS

A Division of Stardom Alliance
105-501 Silverside Road Wilmington, DE 19809, USA

www.stardombooks.com

Stardom Books, United States
Stardom Books, India
The author and publishers have made all reasonable efforts to contact copyright-holders for permission, and apologize for any omissions or errors in the form of credits given. Corrections may be made to future editions.

MILES AND MOMENTS
A Voyage to Exquisite Cuisine, Culture and Commerce

Manya Bhatia

p. 266
cm. 13.5 X 21.5

Category: TRV026120: TRAVEL / Special Interest / Culinary
TRV010000: Travel : Essays & Travelogues

ISBN: 978-1-957456-10-2

DEDICATION

I dedicate this book to my "Dadi" who left us when I was just five.
She was my first friend, the one who helped me craft my first
alphabets; which form the words in the book today.
I will cherish my moments with you all my life.

CONTENTS

Acknowledgments   i

SECTION I

    INTRODUCTION   3

1   AUSTRIA   13

2   CZECH REPUBLIC   29

3   ENGLAND   39

4   FRANCE   55

5   GERMANY   67

6   GREECE   83

7   ITALY   101

8   NORWAY   119

9   RUSSIA   131

10   SWITZERLAND   145

11   TURKEY   161

SECTION II

12   CANADA   175

13   USA   193

SECTION III

14	DUBAI	213
15	HONG KONG	227
16	SINGAPORE	237
	CONCLUSION	251

ACKNOWLEDGMENTS

When I first started writing this book, I never thought that a simple attempt at revisiting my old memories would end up taking shape into a book which blended commerce, culture, and cuisine, all my areas of interest. Looking back at it now this experience has helped me grow as an individual. The long hours of research have given me a new appreciation and greater understanding of history and its influence on culture. It has helped me expand my knowledge base and has done a great job at making me hungry.

I would like to start by thanking my parents, for being the best support system a girl could ask for. My mother for being my best friend, staying up with me on late nights with ready snacks and also for lending me her travel journals which helped in the writing of this book. My father for always giving me the best advice, for going through my manuscript and suggesting edits and for providing his unsolicited opinion. Without him, my book would not have taken shape.

My dog Zuzu for always making me laugh whenever I am stressed and for giving me the best cuddles.

To my two best friends, Shreya and Srishti, for always telling me to sleep on time and for making me smile.

My Nani and Nanu; for their love and affection; they have always encouraged me through ups and downs.

I would also like to express my gratitude to my alma mater - Amity School, Saket; for building confidence and conviction in me to attempt this book.

And lastly to my editors for making this possible.

Hopefully, this book is a beginning; I have had memorable experiences traveling through my own Incredible India; which I hope to bring alive someday.

SECTION I

INTRODUCTION

"All that is gold does not glitter,
Not all those who wander are lost;
The old that is strong does not wither,
Deep roots are not reached by the frost.

From the ashes a fire shall be woken,
A light from the shadows shall spring;
Renewed shall be blade that was broken,
The crownless again shall be king."

— J.R.R. Tolkien, The Fellowship of the Ring

The May of 2021. We have completed over one year of living with the pandemic, hopefully, a once-in-a-lifetime event that disrupted the world. I have just achieved the unthinkable, I completed and cleared my class X without setting foot in the school for my studies.

Another academic year has begun, and yet unlike like all those years prior, we are going to spend the summers at home, locked in for our own safety.

I am seated at my table, looking out the window. My earphones are plugged in, and I'm listening to my go-to Spotify playlist. The weather is hot, and it has drizzled a bit, but the humming air conditioner is the only friend who is keeping me cheerful and cool. The cool air is soothing the furrows on my brow. It was a strange vein of thought as my gaze cut across to the table, and I smiled.

There was a photograph of my parents and me smiling wildly at the camera in front of the Louvre. I certainly was not locked away by an evil relative. I am no Rapunzel on that count. My parents are my absolute heroes. I look at another image of my father and me. I have inherited a lot of things from him, one of them being my temperament and the other being our love for marketing and commerce. I knew long before the weight of these choices that I wanted to be different, maybe a concoction of my father, a marketer and a business executive, and my mother – an ardent pet lover and a xenophile with an interest in international culture, and bring my own flavor to it – willingness to express, communicate, share, develop networks, with brands I love, cultures I visit and people I interact. When my classmates spoke of their dreams of becoming doctors, engineers, presidents, and PMs, I told people, when asked, that I wanted to be different. The "different" has taken many avatars as I moved through my experiences – an architect, a fashion designer, a psychologist, a businesswoman, a travel blogger, and a brand and communications specialist.

My need to be "wholesome in my experiences and not restricted to parts" of understanding is what made the places I visited stand out differently, and it fuelled my desire to look at my experiences of travel through multiple lenses.

A great part of who I am is shaped by my travel experiences, both in India, my home country, and more so internationally. Who's complaining? Not me. As a 17-year-old, I understand how blessed I am to have seen 20+ countries across the American, European, and Asian continents experiencing history, culture, people, and cuisine. These are also some of the topics that I have been interested to learn more about throughout my life. Traveling around the world has favored my interest in commerce. During my travels, I have seen many photoholics and selenophiles. The tourist spots and picturesque sights attract them. They rush to these places, take snaps to post them on Instagram, and document their travels in vlogs. My love for these sights is as much as the next person. However, I was always keener on learning the history and commerce of a place.

What made a city like it is today? How did they amass so much wealth that they could build such marvels? I was equally enamored to find businesses that existed for centuries and carried a legacy that very few possess; I was fascinated by their history and prospects. Some of them were failing, but they had interesting stories to tell. My father and I have looked and found such stories in our many travels. It broadened my knowledge.

> *"Travel is fatal to prejudice, bigotry, and narrow-mindedness, and many of our people need it sorely on these accounts. Broad, wholesome, charitable views of men and things cannot be acquired by vegetating in one little corner of the earth all one's lifetime."* — Mark Twain, The Innocents Abroad / Roughing It.

Suddenly a refrain hit my ears: *I'm sitting here, I miss the power; I'd like to go out, taking a shower; But there is a heavy cloud inside my head; I feel so tired, put myself into bed; Well, nothing ever happens, and I wonder; Isolation is not good for me, Isolation, I don't want to sit on a lemon tree...* A notification sound chimed, slowly dimming the sound of the song. I continued humming to *Lemon Tree* by Fool's Garden as I saw that it was a WhatsApp notification. One of my friends had sent a video. It was drone footage of the city we lived in. I immediately opened the link and was stunned for the next few minutes. The streets were empty of people and vehicles. The city's edifices seemed to stand as lonely watchtowers patrolling the absence of mankind. We were locked within them and warned of the world outside. In our absence, I saw my city in a new light. It looked like a ghost town. But did it have to look so stunning in its silence? The drone footage only exacerbated my sense of being rooted. I closed the video, and my Spotify playlist resumed in the absence of the video. It was as if it had sensed my mood. A few picks on a morose-sounding guitar sounded as the lyrics began at a trice: *Blackbird singing in the dead of night; Take these broken wings and learn to fly; All your life, you were only waiting for this moment to arise...* As The Beatles crooned on about the blackbird, it could not help but make me feel trapped.

I am aware of the many underpinnings behind the song and the message of racial equality that inspired Paul McCartney to write that song. However, for that moment, that song became a personal metaphor. Dear reader, I ask for your allowance for a young girl's indulgence. At that moment, I felt like a blackbird upon whom a gilded existence was imposed. It was a long since I was not traveling in the summer. Like most people, I love to travel. Seeing new places, experiencing different cultures, and learning about different lifestyles is what travel is all about. However, travel can also be a great learning experience. Whether you're traveling for business or pleasure, you can learn a lot about yourself and your world. Oh, how I wish I were writing this from a quiet corner in Italy! But I cannot. So, I did what one would do; I revisited my travel journal.

Since my childhood, I have been traveling the world, and it has taught me so much. My mother and I pen down our experiences in a travel diary. As I started traveling at quite a young age, most of the cities I visited initially were viewed from a perspective of "fun." But as I grew up, I learned that one of the most important things I need to practice is how to open up my mind. I have been exposed to so many different cultures and lifestyles that made me more tolerant and understanding of others.

Today, I can see the differences play out in news channels and social media platforms. My travels have made me more welcoming as I have seen others welcome me and teach me hospitality and generosity. I have learned that there is more than one way to live and that we can all learn from each other. I am now more open-minded than ever, and I believe that this is one of the most valuable lessons I have learned from traveling. It was so important for me to immortalize these experiences and the lessons, so I learned to write them down. Having done that, I can now intersperse them with recent education on economics and public policy to see how history, culture, and location influenced the commerce of these countries /cities and further shaped the cuisine. One of the best things about traveling the world is that you get to experience so many different cultures.

It can be a bit overwhelming at first, but you can learn a lot if you open yourself up to it. When I traveled to Hong Kong, I was excited to try all the different foods and learn about the culture. However, I was also nervous because I didn't know anything about etiquette. But instead of being afraid of making mistakes, I tried to be as open as possible and go with the flow. In the end, I had an amazing time and learned so much about the place. Since then, I've traveled to many different countries, and I've learned something new each time.

Travelling has taught me a lot, but one of the most important things it has taught me is how to get out of my comfort zone. As a small child, I used to be a very shy person, and I would never have dreamed of doing some of my things. But traveling has shown me that there is so much more to life than my little comfort zone and that it is worth getting out there and exploring. It has also taught me that I am a lot braver than I thought and can handle anything that comes my way. Traveling is an excellent way to learn more about yourself and your world. By opening yourself up to new experiences and cultures, you can better understand who you are and what you want out of life. In addition to learning more about yourself, traveling can also teach you a great deal about the world around you. By immersing yourself in different cultures, you can learn about their customs, traditions, and beliefs. This can help you develop a greater appreciation for the world and many other peoples. Travelling can be a great way to relax and unwind from the stresses of everyday life. It can also be an opportunity to explore new places and meet new people.

One of the best ways to immerse and learn about other cultures is to enjoy the different cuisines in other countries. There are few better representative examples of a culture and its history than its cuisine. The ingredients, cooking methods, and even the presentation of a dish can offer insight into the people who created it. For example, spice in Indian cuisine likely has its roots in the country's history of being a major stop on the spice trade routes. Similarly, the popularity of seafood in Japan can be traced back to the island nation's dependence on the sea for trade and food.

Understanding a culture's cuisine can give us a greater understanding of the culture as a whole.

In nearly every culture, food is more than just sustenance. It's a way to connect with others, show love, and celebrate special occasions. For many people, food is a key part of their identity. It can be a source of pride, and sharing it with others is a way to show off your culture. A country's cuisine is a reflection of its history and culture. The ingredients, cooking methods, and flavors are all influenced by the people and events that have shaped that country's past. The dishes you enjoy today result from centuries of culinary traditions being passed down from generation to generation.

The world has become smaller and more connected, and the cuisine has changed to reflect this. In the past, the cooking was heavily based on what was available in a certain region. This is no longer the case as people can get ingredients from across the world. This has led to a fusion of cuisines where multiple cultures are represented in one dish. As more and more people move to different countries, they bring their culinary traditions. This has led to a variety of cuisines being represented in most countries. For example, in the United States, you can find dishes from Mexican, Italian, Chinese, Japanese, and Indian cuisine. This diversity is a reflection of the country's history and culture. My memories of the many delicious dishes have me salivating.

It was at this a sprightly tune shook me out of my reverie.

I stepped out of the confines of my room to make myself a summer refresher when I picked up my father listening to the mellifluous *Yun Hi Chala Chal* from the movie *Swades*. Generally, my taste in music has been different, but this time I was attracted to the lyrics. The song talked of the wonders of home for the lost traveler, but I felt the wanderlust in my bones. I wanted to travel once more. I remembered the sights, the smells, and the sounds. I was lost in a trice. The memories replayed themselves in my head. However, there is always one drawback to nostalgia. The present will never be as rosy as the past. My present was further exacerbated by the fact that I was a bit lost in lockdown. I was struck with a strange affliction.

It was the opposite of homesickness. I wanted to see the world, hear the stories, and taste the delights they hid. I realized I was lost when my mother shook me and handed me my favorite Goan iced tea. We had an impromptu sat down, and the discussion quickly moved to our holidays in the years gone by. I broached upon my musings of that day. I told my parents how I felt trapped and wished to go again into the world. My father told me we could not be sure when we will be allowed to travel. And then he put this interesting proposition to me. **"Why don't you write about it?"**

He explained how there is something special about looking back on old memories. Whether it's flipping through a photo album, watching home videos, or simply thinking about a past event, reliving memories can be a source of happiness. It can be a way to connect with loved ones, both past and present. It can be a way to remember who we are and where we have been. It can be a way to reflect on our lives and all that we've experienced. Whatever the reason, reliving memories is a cherished part of life. We all have memories that we cherish and never want to forget. What if there was a way to keep those memories alive forever? Books are the perfect way to do just that! By creating a travel book, I could document my most precious memories and look back on them time and time again. He asked me to pen down my thoughts and memories and thus author a travelogue. I agreed with enthusiasm.

However, I drew a blank when I sat at my desk about 30-40 minutes later. I was not sure where I should begin and where I should end. What should I write about? After an aimless romp through my thoughts, I took a blank sheet of paper. I plugged in my earphones and resumed my playlist.

Then I wrote down and planned what I wanted to say in this book. I wanted this travelogue to be personal while being interesting to the reader. One idea was to write about what other travelogues missed. However, upon greater reflection, I realized that I did not want to write a book about the sights to see or fill in a vacancy. I wanted my book to do more. I cannot profess to be the be-all and end-all virtuoso traveler.

It was then the thought hit that I should tell the stories I heard and saw in the cities I traveled. My recent interests in economics and commerce have encouraged me to see my travels from a different lens. I wanted to tell the stories of businesses that prospered in a town. I wanted to say the legacies of some of these businesses and how they are still successful or failing today. It is not to say that I eschewed writing about the popular places to be unique. Some of these spots are deservedly tourist hotspots. You may have seen them in pictures and videos, but their true majesty can only be experienced in person. Dear reader, as your scribe, I have tried to capture my feelings of that majesty in the following pages. I have also dedicated time to revisit some of the exquisite delicacies these places offer. But I have spent most of these pages looking at the commerce within these cities. Why? You may ask. I can assure you that it goes beyond the fact that I am an economics and commerce student and that my interest lies in this area. Commerce has long been an indicator of culture and history. It is one of the oldest human activities and has been a part of every human society. For example, the ancient Egyptians had a thriving trade in goods and services. This allowed them to create a prosperous society and a rich culture. Today, trade is still a vital part of every culture and society. It plays a role in the economy, politics, and even social interactions.

Commerce has always been a reflection of the culture and history of the people. It can be seen in the way that people trade with each other, the way that they use money, and the way that they produce goods. All of these things reveal the values and beliefs of a society. For example, people would trade goods and services in ancient societies using barter. This showed that they valued what they had to offer and that they were willing to trade for other things that they needed. In modern society, people use money to buy and sell goods. This shows that we value what we can get for our money and are willing to work for it.

Commerce is the activity of buying and selling goods and services. It is the lifeblood of any society, as it allows people to trade what they have for what they need.

Throughout history, commerce has been the driving force behind the rise and fall of civilizations. It has brought people together and torn them apart. It has created wealth and poverty. It has been a force for good and evil. Today, commerce continues to reveal the culture and history of our world. Every transaction is a snapshot of the people's values, beliefs, and traditions. Through commerce, we can see the interconnectedness of our world and the shared humanity that bind us all together.

As I write this, dear reader, my playlist has shuffled to *Travel*, a song by Bolbbalgan4, a South Korean musical act. The chorus asks how she wants to travel to cities like London, New York, and Paris and get lost in the city like a bird flying free in her youth. So, dear reader, in what seemed like a perfect circle to round off my thoughts here, I hope to take you on a journey with me. Let us fly like birds, and I shall give you the city's best view through the prism of its culture, commerce, and cuisine.

1

AUSTRIA

"The hills are alive with the sound of music, with songs they have sung for a thousand years. The hills fill my heart with the sound of music. My heart wants to sing every song it hears."
— Maria in The Sound of Music

My earliest memories as a child include watching many great movies with my parents. One such movie was The Sound of Music. If you have watched this classic musical, you know that along with the plot, the cast, and fantastic songs, the thing that really hooks you to the movie is its setting and location. The first time I saw Austria was in this particular movie. I could not help but notice how the place looked like it was out of a fairy-tale; knowing that the site was 100% real was another joy. So, you can imagine my excitement when we actually got to visit the place.

Austria is a landlocked country surrounded by Germany, Switzerland, Italy, Hungary, and the Czech Republic. I mean, What a fantastic line-up!

Bastionsgarten – used as a set in Sound of Music

I was shocked to find out how many famous things, people, and practices have originated in Austria. Don't believe me? I'll give you a tour. Let's start with the basics: Beverages.

Dietrich Mateschitz visited Thailand in 1982. He was an entrepreneur at heart, so he wasn't just touring around Thailand. He was looking for opportunities. He was particularly looking for something to cure his jetlag. His fortune changed when he discovered an energy drink called 'Krating Daeng.' Although they are different entities, Dietrich Mateschitz collaborated with the Yoovidhya family, the founders of the Krating Daeng, to create Red

Bull. The formula was adjusted to meet the western taste palate. The Yoovidhya family still owns 51% of Red bull.

How about Europe's most famous pastry, the croissant? When you hear the word croissant, you instinctively picture a tiny café in Paris. A coffee cup, fruit bowl, and a croissant are on the table waiting to be devoured. All that is nice, of course. But croissant isn't French. Croissant comes from Vienna, the capital city of Austria. In Paris, croissants and other pasties are called Viennoiseries.[1]

But croissants aren't the only thing to emerge out of Vienna. This beautiful city has been home to great musicians, like Mozart. Don't be surprised if you happen to hear 'Eine kleine Nachtmusik' in your mind during the entirety of the tour. It is as if it was composed to describe the beauty of Vienna. Mozart began as a pianist in Vienna; he later became the finest keyboardist in Vienna.

Soon, he started composing, and his work was being performed in all of German-speaking Europe. This brought fame to Mozart. Mozart's journey in Austria is important because it is evidence of how much of a cultural hub Austria had become. Musicians and artists from all over the world came to Austria. The best example is Beethoven, who wasn't an Austrian but lived in Vienna for most of his life. The places he lived in are now established as museums open to the public. But one can imagine his contribution to establishing Vienna and Austria as a cultural hub by extension.

Tourism is certainly the pillar of the Austrian economy. Artists like Mozart, Beethoven, Franz Liszt, Strauss (both junior and senior), Schoenberg, Josef Haydn, and Franz Schubert were all from Austria. They have contributed a great deal of value to the tourism industry in Austria as there are a lot of museums, theatres, and other great sources of entertainment dedicated to them. People from all over the world visit Austria in hopes of sighting some evidence of their existence. Along with such artists, Vienna has housed several intellectuals like Sigmund Freud and Leon Trotsky.

Austria has a long and proud history of art and culture.

---

[1] https://theworldpursuit.com/facts-about-austria/

Over the years, many great artists have called Austria home, including Mozart, Beethoven, and Schiele. Today, Austria is home to a number of world-renowned museums, including the Museum of Fine Arts in Vienna, the Leopold Museum, and the Albertina. These museums offer visitors the opportunity to experience the very best of Austrian art and culture.

If you're looking for the best museums in Austria, you can't go wrong with the Albertina. This world-renowned museum houses one of the largest and most important collections of graphic art in the world. From ancient to modern times, Albertina's collection spans a wide range of styles and periods. With over a million items in its collection, there's something for everyone at the Albertina.

In addition to its world-class collection, the Albertina is also known for its beautiful architecture. The museum is housed in a grandiose building that was once the palace of Duke Albert of Sachsen-Teschen. Visitors can admire the palace's stunning neoclassical facade and grandiose interiors as they take in the building.

The Belvedere is a magnificent palace located in Vienna, Austria. It was built in the early 18th century for Prince Eugene of Savoy, and today it houses one of the world's finest collections of art. The palace and its grounds are beautifully landscaped, and the views from the Belvedere are simply breathtaking. The Belvedere is home to a wide variety of art, from Medieval tapestries to 18th-century paintings.

The most famous painting in the collection is "The Kiss" by Gustav Klimt. Other highlights include works by Leonardo da Vinci, Raphael, Rembrandt, and Vincent van Gogh. The Hofburg Palace is one of the best museums in Austria. It is the former imperial palace of the Habsburg dynasty, and it now houses a large collection of art and artifacts from that era. The palace is also home to the Austrian National Library, which is one of the largest libraries in the world. Visitors can take a tour of the palace, or they can explore the museum on their own.

The Kunsthistorisches Museum is one of the best museums in

Austria. Located in Vienna, it is home to an extensive collection of art from the Middle Ages to the present. The museum also has a large number of Egyptian and Greek artifacts. The Kunsthistorisches Museum is a must-see for anyone interested in art or history.

Kunsthistorisches Museum

The Leopold Museum is home to one of the largest collections of modern Austrian art, with over 5,000 paintings, sculptures, drawings, and photographs.

The museum also has a number of interactive exhibits, making it a great choice for both adults and children. And if you get hungry during your visit, the museum has its own cafe which serves up some delicious Austrian cuisine.

The Vienna Museum is the largest and most visited museum in Austria. It is located in the city of Vienna and is home to over 8 million artifacts and artworks. The museum was founded in 1891 and is one of the most important cultural institutions in the country. The Vienna Museum is known for its collections of Austrian art, history, and culture. It also has a large collection of international art.

The Museum of Modern Art houses a collection of over 200,000 modern and contemporary artworks, making it one of the largest of its kind in Europe. The museum has an impressive collection of paintings, sculptures, installations, and photographs, which are displayed across its four floors. Highlights include works by world-renowned artists such as Pablo Picasso, Salvador Dali, and Andy Warhol. Austria was a part of the dual monarchy: The Austro-Hungarian empire. It had about 2 million inhabitants then. The Austro-Hungarian empire was the second-largest country in Europe and crucial for Austria's development. The Austro-Hungarian empire gave rise to the third largest manufacturing base.

Once the empire started to modernize, there was an emergence of railroads that connected cities, expanding Austria's population. Vienna was home to notorious coffee houses. What began with good intentions eventually became a hub for illegal trade. To bring this to an end, The Vienna Stock Exchange was founded during the reign of Empress Maria Theresa. The Vienna Stock Exchange or 'Wiener Börse' is one of the oldest stock exchanges which recently merged with CEESEG AG to reduce its expenses. The Austrian National Bank was also founded during the Austro-Hungarian era, with offices in Vienna and Budapest. These things brought significant changes to Austria, especially in the financial sector.

There were four most dominant industries in the Austro-Hungarian empire: the Automotive Industry, the Locomotive industry, the electrical and electronics industry, and lastly, the aeronautic industry. These industries have contributed largely to the economy of Vienna, especially electrical machinery, oil processing, metal products, cement works, and brickmaking. Vienna accounts for half of Austria's employment, thanks to the service industries. Vienna's Trade Fair also contributes largely to its economy. It takes place twice a year and enables people from Europe and overseas to buy and sell products. The city is also helped by its superb transportation systems—the city's railways as one of the main arteries of regional and international travel. Vienna's airport also can accommodate 30 flights per hour.

I had the chance to visit the stunning Kunsthistorisches Museum. This museum is among the leading art museums globally, with an impressive fine art collection. It has works from Van Dyck and Rubens and houses the world's most extensive Bruegel collection. The granite, marble, and stucco interior of the building are evidence of impeccable Austro-Hungarian designs. One can spend months together just touring the museums of Vienna. As much as I'd have liked that, we minimized our list of museums to four, including this one. The Beethoven Museum was the next one on our list; it is housed in the historic building where the great composer wrote the Heiligenstadt Testament.

One of the exhibits is a letter addressed to Beethoven's brother but was never sent. Beethoven despaired about his loss of hearing and failing health in that letter.

One of the most magnificent museums is the Natural History Museum, Vienna. It is one of the most important natural history museums worldwide. The museum is also a research center highlighting Vienna's importance to research and development. In 2014, 40k people were employed in the R&D department. Along with being the cultural hub of Europe, Vienna has also been the pivot of Austria for life sciences, education, and business. The Natural History Museum is a remarkable example. It has more than 100,000 objects. The scientists researching there have 30 million things available to them. Personally, I'm not a fan of insects and reptiles. So, the gigantic spider had me running for my life at the sight of it! But besides that, it was a wonderful experience.

Another place worth visiting is the Schönbrunn Palace. The palace was built using the Baroque style. It has more than 1400 rooms, including the one that Empress Maria Theresa used. Her influence and the sheer might of her reign can be felt in the air of Vienna. Everything about the Schönbrunn palace was extravagant. Almost movie-like. The dining room, the way food was brought in and taken out, the richness of tapestry, everything was quite interesting. In addition to this, the Schönbrunn Park and Gardens is another must-see. It is designated as a UNESCO World Heritage Site and adds value to the tourism sector of Vienna.

The food in Vienna was fantastic. Viennese food has been repping as Austrian food for centuries. However, lately, some regions of Austria have developed their own distinct way of cooking. Nevertheless, the culinary culture of Vienna is something to talk about. My mouth still waters, thinking of tender and flavoury wiener schnitzel. Typically, wiener schnitzel is made of veal meat coated in flour and fried; We alternated with chicken and potatoes. Though it sounds pretty simple, the flavors were memorable. The best way to have it is to squeeze a lemon on it! And oh, the potatoes, they are one of a kind.

One can really taste Vienna's authenticity and flavor in this potato salad. This salad is prepared in a vinegar mixture rather than a mayonnaise base, unlike other salads.

Käsekrainer is another treat to remember. Globally, it goes by many names like frankfurter, wurst, sausage, or hot dog. But in Vienna, people call it wiener. The correct way to make it is to take a whole baguette, scoop the bread out in the middle. Put a suitable quantity of mustard (must be fresh to avoid a bitter taste) and ketchup, and then stick the wiener inside. I love cheese and always insisted on adding it as a topping. We had it as a quick meal before we went sightseeing, and it was perfect.

Going on to desserts, Viennese food is famous for its huge spread of pastries. I have two favorites under this category. First, we have warm, gooey, jam-filled sweet rolls called 'Buchteln.' When served hot, one feels like the morning sunbeam is melting in one's mouth. The fluffiness of bread and the jam retaining its essence after baking is easier said than done. Second, we have the infamous Apple Strudel or the 'apfelstrudel.' It has been the most popular dish in all of Europe, especially those belonging to the Austro-Hungarian Empire. Apple Strudel is a layered pastry with an apple filling. Many top it off with ice cream or custard. The pie is a bit gooey, which I like. It is also an indication that the apple filling is not overdone. The key here is to make sure that the pastry is relatively thin. While you can get this outside of Austria, most people tend to overdo the apple filling or make the pastry a lot thicker than it should be.

Hallstatt:

Our journey took us to a beautiful little town called Hallstatt that looked like it was out of a storybook. It was as if it was staged to look fictional. Hallstatt is breathtaking. It has exceptional scenic beauty in every direction you look. You may mistake yourself for being stuck in a painting. But Hallstatt is more than a gorgeous-looking toy town. In German, Hallstatt's name stands for 'the place of salt.' The city has been named so because of its salt mines.

While the salt mines have contributed to salt production, there is another reason why the salt mines of Hallstatt have gained fame. The extraordinary preserving powers of salt have kept alive many signs of life dating back to the Neolithic times. In fact, in a recent discovery, archaeologists found traces of human excrement in the mine, which helped determine that people had beer and blue cheese on their menu 2,700 years ago.[2]

Hallstatt's salt mine is still one of the oldest working salt mines globally. It also holds the record of having the oldest industrial pipeline, which transports brine to other Austrian cities. One of the memorable experiences I had in Hallstatt would be of a funicular railway that connects Salzwelten, an ancient salt mine, with the

---

[2] https://www.youtube.com/watch?v=KZb-KRowBDc

subterranean Salt Lake and the Skywalk Hallstatt viewing platform. When the train passed through the salt mine, I felt spooked. There is so much history out there; you can taste it in the air. I was particularly fascinated by the funicular train. I have taken it many times during my time in Europe. It combines many concepts from physics – from how friction is addressed, what gradient one can go on, and what velocity would be able to negate the pull downwards.

The lake is pretty popular in Hallstatt, along with the church and marketplace. One can enjoy a sunbath. I was tempted to swim, but my mother thought otherwise. She forbade me to swim as the 20-22 degrees can be too cold for the average Indian. Or perhaps, she thought I'd drown. Either way, I am yet to swim in Hallstatt's waters, which is something I look forward to doing in the future. I would say the freshwater fish is a must-try at Hallstatt.

Hallstatt

Undoubtedly, Hallstatt's current economy leans on the tourism sector. Even though this market town has a population of just 800, it receives more than a million visitors each year.

Most of the tourists happen to be Chinese. It is so popular among the Chinese that they created a replica of Hallstatt back in China. Hallstatt is famed as the most instagrammable city in the world. It would not be a surprise to see that tourists cannot stay away from the town. However, while these visitors have magnified Hallstatt's economy, but leave disappointed as Hallstatt suffers from over-tourism.

Huge numbers of people pile up every street and crowd the view. It is hard to enjoy the beauty of Hallstatt when such multitudes of people mill about the landscapes. The locals, too, are unhappy with the number of tourists pouring into the town. They claim that "short term visitors swamping the place isn't so great for people who live there."[3]

Salzburg

Just an hour away from Hallstatt lies another incredibly beautiful place called Salzburg. This is the place from The Sound of Music. I was enchanted by the song 'Do Re Mi' from the movie and always wanted to experience the stunning place. I was overjoyed and squealing with excitement when we decided to spend the day at Salzburg taking the Sound of the music tour. A significant part of the song 'Do Re Mi' in The Sound of Music was filmed at the Mirabel Palace Gardens.

I still have fresh memories of running around the open garden reminiscing the film in my mind. My mother and I knew the song, and we enjoyed singing it aloud. Another exciting experience was running in the hedge maze. Our next walk was to Horse Bath. In the movie, Maria and the Von Trapp kids play with water, which is one of my favorite scenes in the film. It was surreal to experience these things in real life. It was as if you were able to jump into your favorite story.

---

[3] https://www.deccanchronicle.com/lifestyle/travel/020819/austrian-town-of-800-receives-1-million-tourists-annually.html

Leopoldskron Palace

Salzburg is also called the Mozart-town. Mozart was born and spent the first 25 years of his life in Salzburg. His house No. 9 Getreidegasse is conserved like a museum. We had the chance to visit the Mozart Footbridge, which is also covered in the movie. There is another bridge full of lovers' locks.

This practice is said to have been inspired by the movie I Want You, where two teen lovers attach a padlock with their names to the bridge and throw the key into a river to symbolize eternal love. Naturally, the bridge attracts several couples as a way to declare their undying love. The movie also featured a famous gazebo, and we looked for it. We were told that initially, the gazebo was in the Leopold Palace, which stands magnificently next to the lake. Then we were told that it was moved to the Hellbrunn Palace Gardens. Both places were worth every minute. The walk in the palace gardens and lazing around in the summer sun was the perfect setting to soak in the Austrian summer.

Salzburg is as beautiful as every other place in Austria. Although, it does share more than one similarity with Hallstatt. Salzburg, too, is known for salt extraction. Salzburg's main sources of income besides salt extraction were gold mining and trade.

The city of Hallein in Salzburg produces more than 72,230 tonnes of salt every year.[4] 'Hall' in German means 'salt,' so it is understood that any city with the name 'hall' has some history involving salt. The Celtics found salt in Hallein and established a community there. The current economy of Salzburg is fuelled by tourism, but it is also home to many international corporations. As Salzburg offers a high quality of life, it attracts numerous companies. To support this, Salzburg also has excellent transportation links, with flights, buses, and trains running every hour of the day. Does work ever feel like work in Salzburg? With all that beauty, I wonder! Salzburg hosts several cultural festivals that attract tourists worldwide, adding to its income. Salzburg is every tourist's dream with fascinating museums, captivating baroque architecture, and stunning palaces.[5]

Innsbruck:

I remember Innsbruck first and foremost for its doner kebap. Innsbruck is full of doner kebab joints, which shows how much people love it there. I agree with them. The tenderness of a lamb filled in a warm pita, filled with lettuce, tomato, onion, yogurt sauce, and chili, is heaven in a bite. A classic doner kebap should ideally have a fresh Pita, the meat should be grilled, preferably in a vertical rotisserie, and the pita should be filled with fresh tomato, lettuce, cabbage, onions (adding a dash of sumac improves the taste), pickled cucumber (for extra flavor) and sauces to taste. For vegetarians, one can just have vegetables. I like mine without the sauces as they drown the essence of meat and vegetables. We enjoyed the Austrian mountains with a cable car ride between Innsbruck and the

---

[4] https://www.salzwelten.at/en/blog/salzburg-saltmine

[5] The economy in city and country Salzburg - SalzburgPORTAL, simply more Salzburg (salzburg-portal.com)

Nordkette, at the heart of the country's nature park. We got out of the car and trekked up the mountain to get a spectacular view of the Alps. It is said you can see Germany from there. Then came the Bergi Ski Jump, which offered a spectacular view. My father told me Zaha Hadid, a famous architect, designed it.

My favorite place in Innsbruck the Swaroski Museum. This place surpassed all my expectations! It is a contemporary art museum where all the installations are made from Swarovski crystals, and they are beautiful! Sadly, you're not going to find out anything about producing Swarovski crystals (which I'm not interested in anyway). Still, you'll enjoy fantastic art, and the gardens are an experience in themselves. The chandelier of grief was beautiful and disorienting at the same time. The sun lit up the crystal cloud and the water feature, and they just glistened outside.

Swarovski Musuem

Innsbruck's economy leans on small and middle-sized businesses. Like all Austrian cities, the city earns quite a lot from tourism. The winter sports facilities are one main attraction of the town.

Austria is a country with such scenic and architectural beauty that one may be forgiven for thinking it came out of a page from a fairy tale. It can be a hotspot for hikers and skiers due to the Alps. However, it is more than that. It possesses a great cultural and artistic heritage. From Mozart to Sound of Music, Austria is a country of sophistication and beauty. As I write this book and reminisce about Austria, I can't help but think of *daffodils, green meadows, skies full of stars, raindrops on roses, whiskers on kittens…these are a few of my favorite things…*

2

CZECH REPUBLIC

"Farther, where strings of rain hang from a little cloud,
Under the hills with an acacia grove
Is Prague.
Above it, a marvelous castle
Shored against a slope in accordance with old rules.
— Czeslaw Milosz

Prague's architectural environment surpasses the majority of the European towns. With each step, there is something new to marvel at. Prague is one of the most beautiful towns I have ever visited, with its narrow cobblestoned streets, the clearest skies, and architecture that transports you back in time.

This is a spot that invites you to sit down and smell the roses when life is tugging you a thousand ways.

Prague, or "Praha," is the Czech Republic's capital and has a timeless air about it. In World War II, the city sustained far less damage than others, and it has since become a major tourist destination. Prague has variously been referred to as the Golden City, the City of a Hundred Spires, and the Heart of Europe. Prague was established on the banks of the Vltava River and consists of five ancient settlements. I have learned from history that The Boii, a Gallic tribe after whom the country of Bohemia was called, initially occupied the territory where Prague now stands.

Národní Museum overlooking Wenceslas Square

My senses were bombarded as I looked up, down, left, and right at the city of Prague. Prague exceeded all expectations, from gazing at vivid hues on Baroque façades to inhaling the fragrances of freshly baked delicacies to hearing the whispers of a language as distinct as its history.

Prague became an imperial city and prospered under the reign of the Holy Roman Emperor, Charles IV (1346 – 1378). The emperor developed Nové Mesto (New Town) for the Czech people and erected the iconic Charles Bridge to unite the cities. The Town Hall in the Old Town was built in 1338. We started our exploration of Prague with the city's most significant and maybe most busy attraction, Prague Castle. The Prague Castle is a massive structure. It's not just a single structure, like a fort or citadel. It's a sprawling complex of structures, many of which are now utilized for offices, museums, and other reasons. Prague Castle provides a variety of tickets that include access to some, several, or all of the many structures. The ticket is good for two days, and believe me when I say that you will need two days to tour the entire castle!

We also visited the St.Vitus Cathedral. This is Prague's equivalent of Westminster Abbey in London. It's not simply a house of worship; it's also where the Czech royalty's coronations, marriages, and burials take place! The initial church in this location was established in 925 CE, and in 1060 CE it was transformed into a Romanesque Basilica. The current church's building began in 1344 CE but was completed only in 1929 CE after being abandoned for centuries and finally restarted in the late 1800s! The main nave of the Cathedral is now encircled by various chapels. Stained glass windows from the Neo-Gothic era are breathtaking. This is also Europe's oldest cathedral. Until 1997, The cathedral, which is part of the Prague Castle complex and contains the tombs of many Bohemian kings and Holy Roman Emperors, is owned by the Czech government as part of the Prague Castle complex. It was constructed around a great tower and a transept, which was enclosed by a temporary wall. A timber-roofed structure stood in the place of a three-aisled nave-to-be-built, and services were held separately from the choir's interior. Some chapels are located just behind the altar and are adorned with beautiful artwork. The Last Judgement Mosaic on Golden Gate is one such breathtaking artwork. It's simply opulent and stunning! St. George's Basilica was our next stop following St.Vitus Cathedral.

It is the second church to be built in Prague Castle after St.Vitus Cathedral. Despite the fact that St.Vitus Cathedral contains ancient murals, it was far too crowded for me to appreciate them. On the other side, St. George's Basilica drew just a quarter of the attendance. Though the first church was built in 920 CE by Prince Vratislav I, the current construction is from the early 13th century, and the Baroque sections are from the 18th century. The partially fading paintings are a sight to behold for any history buff. There's a little cafe on the way to Golden Lane, and the tomato hummus panini here was delicious! It appears that Prague has a sizable vegetarian/vegan population, as the vegetarian cuisine selections are rather good and excellent!

When I visited Charles Bridge which connects Prague's Old Town to the Little Quarter, I was enraptured by its sight. It was one of my most wonderful experiences in the city. I felt like I'd journeyed hundreds of years back in time as I strolled across the Vltava River and studied the myriad surrounding attractions. Because of the Charles Bridge's central location, it's simple to combine your stroll with one of the adjacent areas, making for an amazing day. The Charles Bridge is one of Prague's most well-known landmarks, situated in the heart of a city noted for its Gothic and Baroque architecture. It is the oldest bridge across the Vltava River and the second-oldest bridge in the country. Prague is brimming with stunning architecture. You can just stroll around and be amazed by your surroundings, especially if you're walking around downtown. We discovered this to our great joy as we toured the city's streets. We came across a plethora of eccentric sculptures and public art. Aside from this, there were other wonderful old buildings and street artworks to see. Obviously, the most important face of Prague is Charles Bridge. Under King Charles' reign, the Charles Bridge was constructed between 1357 and 1402. From 1683 through 1928, 30 statues of various saints and Gods were put here. The oldest of these sculptures were transported to a secure location throughout time to safeguard them from nature and man! When we went to see this sculpture of John of Nepomuk, which is the oldest of the statues now on the bridge, it was fairly overcast. Its green and gold color contrasted magnificently with the grey sky! It is made of sandstone blocks, with fortified towers at either end - the Lesser Town Bridge Towers and the Old Town Bridge Tower.

The Golden Lane was our next stop. This is to gain a sense of how life might have been for an average guy in Prague a few centuries ago. While the lower story is packed with restored antique dwellings, the upper floor features a display of warrior weapons and metal costumes. This street was once known as Gold Smith's Lane, and it was once home to Gold Smiths. Other castle personnel, including as guards, gatekeepers, and others, afterward made their houses here.

People here were aware of how attractive and unusual their modest buildings were after WWII, since huge scale, enormous houses and flats were being built at the time. They welcomed visitors on occasion and rented out their homes to painters, authors, and others. This is the final remembrance of life at that time period. The government purchased all of the houses on this street in 1953 in order to keep it as it is forever!

My next stop was the astronomical clock. As I stood there with millions of other visitors witnessing a show in the heart of Prague's Old Town Square, I was lost in time. The oldest working clock - the Astronomical Clock, one of Prague's top attractions – was being prepared to ring the bell. The entire ceremony is done in 45 seconds when the Twelve Apostles parade.

It's not just a show-stopper, but also a little planetarium in itself. There's an astronomical dial with the sun, moon, and universe, a zodiac circle with stars and planets, and a calendar dial, among other things.

The Astronomical Clock isn't the only attraction in the Old Town. The Old Town Hall, a magnificent structure, is located in the middle of Old Town Square. Although they're designed to be highly touristic, look for vintage vehicle rides/tours, tuk-tuks, or hop-on-hop-off buses that offer you the topography of the region. Alternatively, if you're like me, you'll simply walk a lot as you would everywhere in Europe, preferably with a local as part of a tour or otherwise. I climbed the 70-meter-high tower to get a better view of the 1000-year-old skyline, and you'll see why Prague is known as "The Golden City of Thousand Spires."

Heritage Car Drive in Prague

Prague is a unique city. When I first walked into the Lucerna Palace, I noticed a group of individuals standing in front of (or, better still, beneath) a statue. Lucerna Palace is one of the city's most distinctive structures, including stores, a cinema, and theaters in the basement. But it's the presence of a provocative monument that fascinates me. The artist David Cerney produced an upside-down statue of a monarch riding his horse. It appears to be a reference to the Saint Wenceslas monument in Wenceslas Square. Locals, on the other hand, claim that this monument, dubbed Kun, is a mockery of former Czech President Vaclav Klaus.

Prague is home to some of the most beautiful buildings in the world. I see buildings in every architectural style as I travel down the street, from Baroque to Renaissance, Art Nouveau to Gothic. Prague is a beautiful city to wander around, and there are many activities to do there. Every stroll, no matter how long or short, comes to a halt in front of a sculpture or a structure. The Municipal Library was one of the most amazing visits I made. If you are a bibliophile, the sculpture within the Library will appeal to you. "Idiom" is its name, and it seems like a never-ending tower.

Prague is not only about the peculiarities of architecture. When you come to the city's most famous locations, it's more of a sense of accomplishment. The vitality of Wenceslas Square; the Astronomical Clock, with all the people's fingers pointing to the clock's fingers; and, of course, the Charles Bridge, with its incessant comings and goings.

To Prague's sacral architecture, Renaissance chateaux, gothic castles, and medieval villages, the large colorful stroll within the Karltejn and Kivoklát castles, gigantic walls full of paintings and art, and a huge part of books were breathtaking. The Royal Chapel of Angels' excellent kaleidoscopic artwork depicting angels wielding torture devices drew my attention the most. I also visited the fascinating world heritage monuments and the old city of Cesky Krumlov. The location included a variety of activities, including tours of the Cesky Krumlov Castle, which included a huge Rococo-style park, five courts, and spectacular buildings and constructions.

"What do you anticipate eating in Prague?" Yes, there is a common theme in Prague cuisine that incorporates beer and pig. There's more to it than that, though. I found a few favorite places and dishes in Prague. Trdelnk, a chimney cake made by coating and frying dough around a stick to a golden-brown crust, rolling in cinnamon sugar, applying butter, and adding other ingredients, was one of the best dishes I had in Prague. The spectacle of this preparation was as enthralling as the delicacy itself, and it provided an intriguing glimpse into Hungarian culture that captivated the people of Prague.

The Palacinky was another delicious dinner that combined sweetness with a variety of toppings such as whipped cream, jam, ice cream, almonds, chocolates, cheese, and a fruity touch for a perfect bite. With its combination of diverse veggies, rice, and pork, the basic yet attractive décor of Bibimbap, a Korean-inspired food, was intriguing. The cuisine was the greatest I'd ever eaten at that price point, so I'm curious if that's why it's so popular. We stayed in Ambassador Zlata Husa's Hotel on Wenceslas Square, the most exciting spot in town and a must-see for all visitors.

The La Boutique Della Pizza, across the street from the hotel, created wonderful dough and some of the tastiest pizza and Tiramisu I've ever tasted.

My ears and my tastebuds very much remember the melody of jazz-laden Prague and the taste of every delicacy. And my sincerity as a student allowed me to recognize the economy of this precious land. According to Stalin's development philosophy of planned interdependence, all communist nations' economies were inextricably connected to the Soviet Union's.

The "Velvet Revolution" of 1989 provided an opportunity for significant and long-term political and economic transformation. Following the shock therapy dubbed the "great bang" in January 1991 by the International Monetary Fund (IMF), signs of economic rebound began to emerge. Since then, consistent liberalization and prudent economic management have resulted in the abolition of 95 percent of all price controls, low unemployment, a positive balance of payments position, a stable exchange rate, a shift of exports from former communist economic bloc markets to Western Europe, and relatively low foreign debt. Inflation has been higher in certain countries than in others. Two of the government's top concerns have been stringent economic measures and providing a favorable environment for new investment in the country. In late 1995, the Czech crown became completely convertible for most business purposes.

The government has changed the legislative and administrative system controlling investment in order to promote the economy and attract international partners. With the disintegration of the Soviet Union, the country, which had been heavily reliant on exports to the USSR, was forced to undergo a drastic shift in economic outlook: away from the East and toward the West. This needed the reorganization of existing banking and telecommunications infrastructure, as well as the adaptation of business laws and procedures to Western norms. To reduce reliance on a single major partner even further, successive Czech administrations have welcomed U.S. investment (among others) as a counterbalance to the strong economic influence of Western European allies. Prague's GDP per capita is about double that of the Czech Republic, and the city generates more than 21 percent of the national GDP. In terms of GDP per capita/Purchasing Power Parity, Prague is among the 12 richest EU areas. Prague's economy is now built on a variety of industrial sectors. Aircraft engines, diesel engines, refined oil products, electronics, chemicals, food, printing, autos, and other items go into this category and of course tourism.

When I mentioned Jazz earlier, you might have wondered – Really? In Prague? My readers, yes! Though the Czech Republic is likely best known for Bohemian folk music and classical music by composers such as Anton Dvoák, the country also has a rich jazz legacy, with artists such as R. A. Dvorsk and Karel Velebn. Prague is the country's jazz capital, as it hosts the International Jazz Festival and a number of well-known jazz bars. Here are the greatest places to hear this fantastic music genre in the city. Reduta Jazz Club has been a staple of the city's jazz culture for almost 50 years, having opened its doors in 1958 when a group of young jazz artists resolved to create a location where citizens could enjoy outstanding music. The club drew significant names in Czech jazz in its early days, including multi-instrumentalist Karel Velebn, female singer Vlasta Prchová, and double bassist Ludk Hulan. The club is an exquisite and trendy environment with musically themed decor and photos of jazz giants on the walls, as well as plush red sofa seating. The Prague Big Band, an orchestral jazz ensemble, and the Petr Benes Quartet, a contemporary jazz outfit, have both performed at Reduta recently. Jazz has always been at the core of Prague's music culture, thriving even during the city's turbulent periods. Thanks to the luminaries who passed down their heritage and the next generation of artists who have enthusiastically embraced it, jazz is as vibrant and soulful as it has ever been in modern Prague.

Do I dream about Prague still? Yes. Am I still allured by the Czech culture? Also, yes. The alleys, the buildings, the history, the politics, altogether my trip to the Czech Republic was enlightening. They have actually allowed me to look at the world differently. I was not a mere traveler; I held my parents' hands and traveled all around absorbing their culture. I can say very confidently you can learn and have fun at the same time. Each city narrates a tale, once we learn the art of listening, we will be surrounded by the light of knowledge, which is unique.

3

ENGLAND

"When a man is tired of London, he is tired of life; for there is in London all that life can afford." — Samuel Johnson

What is the first image that comes to your mind when you hear the word 'England'? For me, it is tea, the royal family, fish and chips, and of course, the Harrys! Both Potter and Styles! When you hear the word tea, the stereotypical image that forms in your mind is a group of ladies in their dress gowns, sitting in a room with big chandeliers, their backs straight as a pole. They hold the cup's stem with three of their fingers and their little fingers pointing outward. They pick up their cups and take a sip and place the cup back on the saucer in between sips. They could discuss everything from the weather to the ball next week. It is the stereotypical British posh image. The issue lies in tea being considered English, with great fame given to its Yorkshire output. The Yorkshire tea is one of England's more recognizable exports. However, it is also a marker for the country's colonial past and the globalized present. Not many, including some Englishmen, know that Yorkshire tea is actually not grown in Yorkshire.

The Yorkshire Tea is actually a blend of 20 different teas grown across Africa and India. The name comes from where the tea has been blended. What does this mean? Tea has become an inextricable part of English culture. It was even the witness and subject of a political and mercantile protest in Boston that led to the American Revolution and Independence. However, a deeper investigation into colonial history will show how tea was smuggled from China and cultivated in Assam, India. The British encouraged the growth of the tea industry in India. They encouraged the growth but took the produce back home with them. England today is a melting pot of different cultures. It is proof of its rich cultural diversity and its imperialistic past. England may be one out of the four countries that we know as the United Kingdom. However, the country itself has pieces of many nations represented by the people, customs, and cuisines. This diversity is not limited to the major metropoles; it is a feature of every city in the country. Every city in England is a multicultural hub. I am lucky to say that I got to experience the richness of its diversity first-hand. If we were to speak about England's culture, diversity, and economy, there is no better place than the capital city, London.

I have been fortunate enough to visit and experience different cultures in different cities in other countries. They all have their own unique charms. However, if I were to be pushed into making a choice, London would be my favorite city in the world. I am not unusual when it comes to this choice. I have met many people who are equally if not more well-traveled than me; they feel the same way. It has a certain magnetism, and it has the potential of becoming your favorite city whether you have visited it or not. That is the charm of London. (I do promise that the Potter pun was unintended)

London is not only the capital city of both England and the UK but it is also known as the capital city of the world. The city is a global hub and has become a highly influential voice in world politics. Even if Britain has withdrawn from the European Union, I still opine that London is the magnetic core of Europe. The charming essence of London lures in people from all over the world.

People who come to live in London never look back. Many communities, especially the French, have a long-standing history in London. An article published by the BBC describes London as the '6th largest city of France' as more people live in London than in Bordeaux.[6] The French community has mushroomed into every nook and corner of London. It is hardly surprising given that William the Conqueror from Normandy conquered England in 1066 AD. Interestingly, he made the removal of Winchester as the capital of England permanent. You can already guess which city was made the country's permanent capital. London. The French have ever since been a permanent fixture in the English fabric. However, London is called home by people from many more countries other than the French and the natives. There is an obvious explanation for the ongoing popularity of London. The city is a global epicenter for arts, leisure, hospitality, and tourism. Many describe it as a city full of opportunities. It is especially seen as a haven for young people. I must say that London is a go-to for all artistic expeditions as the city is not only brimming with inspiration for artists but is also home to hundreds of art galleries, bookstores, and museums. London's literary history also holds a lot of prominence, as many celebrated minds like Shakespeare have lived and expressed their art in this city.

I remember walking through the streets of London and being surrounded by street art. There can be a pretentious attitude towards graffiti. However, these murals can be museums in themselves. If you are an artist and need inspiration, you need only take a stroll. Every part of London brims with a pulse; there is an inspiration to be found in every nook. This is the reason why people flock to London. They wish to take in some of that magic for themselves. It is why London tourism is a thriving industry. But London wasn't always like this. Initially, London was constructed by the Roman empire to serve as a port and trading settlement. You can blink your eyes and think of the famous nursery rhyme of London Bridge and the River Thames.

---

[6] https://www.bbc.com/news/magazine-18234930

After the Romans built the port, the region became a mercantile destination. It used to be a city full of merchants and guilds.

London Bridge

London has been an important center of global commercial trade ever since. The Roman called the town 'Londinium,' and if we were to speak in terms of real estate, the city was not even 50% in size compared to the London of today. We have to credit the Romans for establishing London in such a way that when we think of it, we instinctively think of it as a city of commerce. Most of Londinium has been lost in the dust. Still, certain places such as the Roman bathhouse, Roman fort, the Roman Amphitheatre, and even Oxford Street in London remain as evidence of the Roman legacy in London. There is little doubt that London has continued to grow. It has multiplied in terms of size and population. Clearly, the Romans have influenced the way London operates commercially. But there are so many other areas where Romans have had a clear impact, like its cuisine.

The pairing of wines with food is one of the cultural and cuisine legacies that England adopted from the Romans. The Romans believed that wine was the unifying force of all their people. It was an essential item on their everyday list. Wine was consumed by merchants, peasants, and enslaved people; no gender or class was excluded from its consumption. Wine was not just a factor in companionship by connecting people; it was also a factor in commercial growth by creating trade opportunities. Since many Romans were living in Britain, it created a demand for cheaper wine on a regular basis. It also promoted learning and sharing the knowledge of winemaking in Britain, slowly giving rise to the wine industry in England.[7]

London's history in trading and commerce has played an enormous role in shaping its cuisine profile. However, no talk of commerce in England would be complete without speaking of the East India Company. East India Company is undoubtedly the greatest corporation formed in the history of the world. Their highly remunerative business could easily compete with the biggest enterprises in the world today. East India Company was based in London and was supported by the Bank of England, alongside Lloyds of London through all stages of its expansion. The result was renewed interest in the commercial and trading aspects in England. There are enough stories of how the East India Company ruled over and exploited many countries, including India. They brought spices like pepper, curry powder[8] and even tea. England became an eminent trading and redistribution center, influencing the expansion of export and imports. The British palate was expanded when the East India Company facilitated the availability and affordability of spices. The quest for new ingredients in the British Empire introduced new dishes, tastes, and flavors into the country's classic food palate. The East India Company permanently changed Britain's Kitchen.

---

[7] https://www.historic-uk.com/HistoryofBritain/Roman-Food-in-Britain/

[8] https://www.bl.uk/learning/timeline/item126721.html

Often, British food is accused of being bland, dull, and basic. They can point to something like the typical English breakfast consisting of baked beans, bread, fried egg, and sausages. It is not the most appetizing fare when you compare it to breakfast dishes across the world. It is fair to recognize that the Indians brought spices to the country; however, initially, spices were exorbitantly expensive to be consumed by everyone. Traditional English dishes comprised potatoes, meat, and vegetables, the only available products for any dish. Thus, it was closer to the Nordics in terms of the palate.

The Romans might be known for bringing wine to Britain, but the fact is they brought more than just wine. The Romans also introduced peas, cabbages, cherries, and more! The Romans were certainly not parsimonious when it came to infrastructure and logistics. They built robust roads that allowed seamless transportation of goods and people across the Roman Empire and the British Isles. Then the Saxons took over and brought along herbs, rippling another unprecedented change in the English palate. Other invaders also brought in their culinary treats, significantly altering the original, ordinary British fare. The earliest indications of British cuisine point to the 9th century. It involved the process of drying fish and smoking techniques, which Danish and Norwegian Vikings introduced in the country. The Normans also played a part in the consumption of some of the common foods, such as mutton and beef. The islanders also adopted their cooking techniques. The importation of food and spices such as cocoa and coffee from South America and herbs from the Far East dramatically influenced the British diet.

While England's traditional foods greatly influence its rich history and cultural heritage, the historical growth of trade and commerce in London throughout the centuries has allowed its modern cuisine to thrive in dynamic diversity. British colonization in the subcontinent of India allowed the diversification of new cultures and influenced fresh cooking ingredients and flavors, thus significantly impacting the preparation of British food.

Curry houses and Indian takeout food have become part of British popular culture. Foreign and cultural influences have improved British cuisine, making London a melting pot of diversity in cooking and population.

If we could revisit the history of tea, you cannot divorce the looming shadow of the East India Company. Tea and its drinking culture were introduced to the country by the East India Company. Before tea was discovered in Assam, it was exclusively grown in China. There was such a demand for tea that they smuggled drugs to China in exchange for it. A Scottish mandarin smuggled tea plants out of China into India, which was later discovered by the members of the East India Company. So, while a Scottish man first smuggled tea, technically, it was a British man who introduced and encouraged the growth of the tea industry in India. India played an enormous part in elevating it to its popularity.

There is a reason for the rapid colonization by the British and the concurrent rise of the British Empire. They subjugated South Asia for their resources and markets. They experimented with pepper, cumin, turmeric, cinnamon, and coriander. These spices are currently used in British cuisine as typical ingredients. However, Britain's food diversity remained a mystery until some significant events changed the landscape. One can trace this to the opening of the first Indian restaurant called Hindoostane Coffee House in 1809. This restaurant was located in London. The Coffee house was set up when spicy food and Indian spices started to pick up steam in the British culture. While it was indeed the first restaurant to be run by an Indian, Indian food such as curry and rice was being served in many other cafes and restaurants before the opening of the Hindoostane Coffee House. The owner, Sake Dean Mahomed, was interested in promoting a cuisine that was a fusion of both Indian and British cooking.

One such example of Anglo-Indian cuisine is kedgeree. Kedgeree is a fancy form of 'Khichri' or 'Khichdi,' one of the best comfort foods in India. Kedgeree had the flavors of Khichri, which is usually made with spices, lentils, and rice, and it was elevated by smoky, salty fish, spiced rice, and hard-boiled eggs. The British colonists who returned home still salivated over this dish and its comfort and pleasure they had left behind.

Hindoostane Coffee House knew that they could fill this niche as Anglo-Indian food was gaining popularity. So they introduced it as a breakfast dish. Today, the London restaurant, Albion Shoreditch, is a great place to eat Kedgeree. Albion specializes in simple, modestly-priced British food. It has a nice woody stylish ambiance where one can experience great food.

It is believed that Anglo-Indian cuisine was born out of the acquaintance that Indian cooks and British homemakers shared during the British Raj. I can only imagine how the conversations must have gone. I can picture both the parties being fascinated by being introduced to a whole new world they must have only heard about in fantastical tales.

Cooking is, in some form, magic. They must have been excited to be introduced to a whole different world with many new ingredients to offer and explore. Since there was a drastic increase in immigration from South Asia, there was also an increase in demand for Indian items and food. This demand led to the creation and establishment of Indian restaurants and other restaurants that offered Anglo-Indian cuisine.

One of the best examples of this exchange is the dish Chicken Tikka Masala. Nobody is sure whether Chicken Tikka Masala originated in India or Britain. Many claim it was invented in Moti Mahal, a famed restaurant in New Delhi. However, it became a household dish in England after establishing many Indian restaurants in the country. It is alleged that the Chicken Tikka was added to a tomato sauce base to cater to the taste and appreciation of the British, and that is how Chicken Tikka Masala was born. We had great Chicken Tikka Masala at Punjab, in Covent Garden. The chef told us that it is the oldest North Indian restaurant in the UK (still serving today). Established in 1946, this place has been run by the same family for four generations. London has a lot to offer. It can give you the heat and excitement of being on vacation.

It will provide you with a multitude of dishes with names you cannot even pronounce. There are places to visit you would have only ever seen in pictures, like Big Ben, The London Eye, etc. These are all the delights this city has to offer. But once you have experienced these sights, smells, and tastes, you will be taken aback by the feeling of homeliness that London will provide. I remember how I did not experience even an iota of homesickness as I munched down a plate of Butter Chicken with Naan bread at the end of a tiring day of exploration. That one juicy bite transported me back to the comfort of being home, even if just for a moment.

One cannot also discount the role of the Spanish conquest of Portugal in the development of England, and specifically London. When Portugal landed in the hands of Spanish rule, religious violence worsened, and Jews were the primary target. The majority of the Jews who fled the place ended up in England, but they brought their rich culture with them.

One of the most recognizable and distinctly British dishes in the world today is fish and chips. When one even says the name of the dish, you will think of England. However, the English had no idea of the existence of such a delicacy until the Jewish refugees landed on their shores and introduced it to them. Jews also opened the way for trading and selling fish in England.[9]

London has held the title of being the financial hub of the world for a while now. The Romans started this reputation by establishing it as a trading hub during their pomp. Then came the advent of the merchants. They crossed the seas to trade with other countries. The merchants set up the Bank of England to financially aid the military services in exploring and conquering new territories to expand and grow their markets. The bank of England has had a significant contribution to the growth of London's status as a financial hub. It took smart steps by introducing policies that fostered and enhanced the position of the city, if not the whole of the United Kingdom. In addition to the bank of England, the establishment and expansion

---

[9] https://www.docksidehhi.com/the-history-of-fish-and-chips/

of HSBC and Barclays, two of the world's most powerful banks today, strengthened its recognition as a financial hub.

The Bank of England is the central bank of the United Kingdom and the model on which most central banks have been based. It was established in 1694 to act as the English Government's banker, and to this day it still acts as the bank for the Government of the United Kingdom. The Bank is one of eight central banks belonging to the European System of Central Banks. The Bank is also sometimes known as the Old Lady of Threadneedle Street, a name taken from its address in the City of London. The Bank of England was instrumental in financing the expansion of the British Empire. It provided loans to the government for wars and other expenditures, and it also invested in British businesses and colonies. The Bank of England financed the expansion of the British Empire through the Opium Wars and the Scramble for Africa. The Opium Wars were fought in order to gain control of the Chinese market for opium.

The Scramble for Africa was a competition between European powers to gain control of African territory. The Bank of England provided loans to the British government in order to finance these imperial ventures. Its first chief purpose was to help finance the war against France. The Bank was also responsible for issuing paper money, and it did so for the first time in 1696. In the following years, the Bank became increasingly involved in the financing of imperial expansion.

It made loans to the government for the purchase of French and Dutch territories, and it also helped to finance the construction of roads, canals, and other infrastructure projects. The Bank played a crucial role in the expansion of the British Empire, and its importance was recognized by the government. In 1844, the Bank was given exclusive note-issuing powers with the passing of the Bank Charter Act.

Today, its primary purpose is to promote the good of the people of the United Kingdom by maintaining monetary and financial stability.

The Bank of England implements monetary policy by setting interest rates and working with commercial banks to influence the supply of money in the economy. Monetary policy is one of the main tools that the Bank of England uses to maintain stability in the economy and keep inflation low.

When I visited London, I had the chance to visit glorious little cafes and coffee houses. I sat in one such café with my parents. They took their time to savor and enjoy a cup of coffee; my attention was on the aesthetics, the interiors, and the clientele that patronized the establishment. It was only recently I learned that coffee houses in London have been more significant than their name suggests.

Many of the great businesses that now support London started from coffee houses. The stockbrokers of the London Stock Exchange first conducted their business in Jonathan's Coffee House. The merchants who used to trade metal also chose coffee houses to trade their wares.

One great example is the development of the Royal Exchange, which later turned into the London Metal Exchange. The metal trade began during the Roman era, and eventually, there were thousands of metal merchants wandering in London waiting for their chance. The Royal Exchange opened its doors in 1571 to enable merchants and assure them a safe place to conduct their trade. Twice, an unfortunate fire incident caused the place to close and reopen. However, in the 19th century, it attracted a huge crowd of merchants to its halls.

Due to the constant rush inside the Royal Exchange Halls, merchants chose a nearby coffee house called the Jerusalem Coffee House as a new base to continue their exchange business. It is said that the coffee house was soon flooded with merchants screaming, "Change!" It is said that there was a tradition where men would draw a circle on the floor full of sawdust and yell 'Change' to imply they were up for business. Those wishing to trade would then assemble around the circle and make their bids. I can only imagine the joy and possibly concern of the owner of that coffee house!

The origin story of the London Metal Exchange is another

inspirational tale. What started in a coffee house is now a premier institution. The London Metal Exchange today is the world's largest metal exchange. It is a global marketplace for metals including steel, aluminum, copper, nickel, lead, zinc, and precious metals. The London Metal Exchange is a leading provider of price discovery and price risk management services for the metals industry. It is home to the world's benchmark contracts for aluminum, copper, lead, nickel, tin, and zinc.

In 1877, the metal traders in the coffee houses and other informal gatherings formalized their arrangement by creating the London Metal Market and Exchange Company. The exchange moved to new premises in 1882 and rapidly expanded in the early 20th century as international trade grew. The LME was formally recognized as a futures exchange in 1925. Today, the LME is a leading international platform for trading metals. It offers contracts for aluminum, copper, lead, nickel, tin, zinc, steel billet, and cobalt. It is the world's largest marketplace for non-ferrous metals. The LME is a member of the London Stock Exchange Group (LSEG). The LME offers two types of trading: ring trading and open-outcry trading. Ring trading is conducted via telephone and open-outcry trading is conducted in the Exchange's ring-dealing room.

The LME is a member of the World Federation of Exchanges (WFE) and is regulated by the Financial Conduct Authority (FCA). It is headquartered in London, England. The LME also provides warehousing facilities for metals. The LME was created in response to the increase in international trade following the Industrial Revolution. Prior to the LME, there was no central marketplace for metals trading. Over time, the LME has evolved into a global marketplace, with trade happening 24 hours a day. Today, the LME is an important part of the global metal industry, with a wide range of metals traded on its platform.

Apart from these institutions, what really helped London is the fact that its native language is English. English also happens to be the dominating language in business, which invited many entrepreneurs, businessmen, and women.

It is another legacy of their imperialistic past. Another supporting factor for London's financial status is its central time zone. London is blessed with a time zone that links the Asian and US markets. It overlaps hours around 27 markets which allows access to global products.

The Romans have contributed in abundance to the shaping of England and especially London. Consider, The English Contract Law; it empowers the contract, which is a binding agreement between two people or services. This sort of consensual agreement can be traced back to the Roman years. English Law is highly important to mention because driven by its original trading approach, it has shaped contract laws worldwide.

One of the main attractions of England is the quality of higher education provided. There are a lot of prestigious business schools in the UK, but two of the most well-known are the London School of Economics and Political Science (LSE) and the London Business School (LBS). Both of these institutions are world-renowned for their high-quality programs and research opportunities.

An education from the London School of Economics and Political Science (LSE) and the London Business School (LBS) offers many advantages. The LSE is consistently ranked as one of the top universities in the world for Economics and Social Sciences, while LBS is in the top 10 business schools. An LSE education provides students with a world-class education in Economics and Social Sciences, preparing them for successful careers in a variety of industries. The school's international reputation means that graduates are highly sought after by employers around the world. The LBS offers an equally world-class education in business, preparing students for leadership roles in a variety of organizations. An LSE or LBS education can provide you with the skills and knowledge necessary to succeed in a number of different industries. The schools' focus on producing well-rounded, globally-minded individuals means that their graduates are in high demand by employers all over the world. In addition to the excellent academic education, one will receive, an LSE or LBS degree will also open up a number of networking opportunities.

However, one cannot just talk about London and England without mentioning Brexit. Brexit has been a hot topic for the past few years. The United Kingdom's vote to leave the European Union has had a big impact on the country, and many are still feeling the effects. While some feel that Brexit was the right move for the UK, others believe that it was a mistake. No matter what the opinion is, there is no denying that Brexit has had a huge impact on England. Prior to Brexit, England was part of the European Union, which allowed for free trade and the movement of people between member states. However, due to disagreements over budget contributions and other issues, the UK voted to leave the EU in 2016. The United Kingdom withdrew from the European Union on 31 January 2020. This has had a number of impacts on the economy, both in the short and long term. In the short term, there has been a decline in the value of the pound, as well as increased inflation and unemployment. The long-term effects are less clear, but some economists predict that there will be a decrease in foreign investment and an overall slowing of the economy. There is also a risk that England will lose its position as a leading financial center.

I must conclude by saying that London is magnificent. The deeper you dig into its history and nature, the more you will be fascinated. I am particularly fascinated by how the confluence of cultures driven by its trading conquests, its cuisine supported by the ingredients, chefs, and recipes brought in from across the globe, and its original forays into commerce through trading has resulted in shaping the London of today.

It is reported that London has at least 250 restaurants for every 10,000 people.[10] The fact that it is a confluence of culture and food and a fulcrum of English has made the migration to England easy and sought after. According to a Deloitte study, "London has the most internationally diverse executive community in the world,

---

[10] London hailed as world's 'city of choice' in quality of life report (cityam.com)

attracting business leaders from 95 nationalities and with alumni working in 134 countries."

Londoners, especially 70% of the female population, have described the city as an inclusive place. They have been presented with great and equal opportunities regardless of gender, ethnicity, race, or sexuality. Additionally, they have carried over a wonderful Roman tradition. They have an effective public transportation system. It is a great setting for social connections and an avenue for a leisurely pace of life. These factors put London at the top of the list of cities with the "highest quality of life."

London Skyline

One can safely conclude that the conquests of Britain earlier and by Britain later and its strong focus on trading (and now service) economy helped shape its ethnicity and diversity. It was also a birthplace of change with the Industrial Revolution's early developments. It also became a beacon by playing host to the emerging centers of education and finance like the London School of Economics, Bank of England, Llyods Exchange, and the London

Metal Exchange. These factors played an important role in attracting people from all over the world to England.

For those who visit it, you will understand that there is a rich history in every nook and cranny of this country. It will inspire you, make you wonder, and leave you reflective for a long time. While you explore it, you will certainly stumble upon something that will make you feel right at home, and personally, I think that is the greatest charm of London.

4

FRANCE

PARIS

Ajoutez deux lettres à Paris, et c'est le paradis
— Jules Renard

(Add two letters to Paris, and it is Paradise)

I do not know about you, but I completely agree with Jules Renard. Paris is Paradise. The general assumption about Paris is that it is the land of fashion. While that is true, Paris is so much more. It has a rich history and is praised for its vibrant culture. It is a multidimensional city with a mesmerizing art scene, a leading economy, and, not to forget, the mouth-watering delicious treats.

When my father told me about our Paris trip, I jumped in excitement. I would again like to thank my parents for giving me this life. I could not have asked for anything better. I visited Paris in 2016 when I was about 11 years old. You might be thinking how a 11-year-old could remember such intricate details from a city. Well, Paris had that effect on me.

I remember everything from greeting Mona Lisa to witnessing the breathtaking view from the top floor of the *Eiffel* Tower. Yes, we managed to get the tickets, and I will explain that in detail later in this chapter.

View from atop the Eiffel Tower

Paris is renowned for its museums, art galleries, and architecture. Start with *Place de la Bastille* if you are in Paris and do not know where to start. That is what we did.

Also known as *Bastille* square, the place marks the start of the French Revolution. If you plan your visit to *Bastille* square, you might catch your favorite artists performing at the Opera Bastille on a lucky day. This square also hosts many festivals and political demonstrations and has become a casual hangout spot. While the north side of the square has a busy nightlife and attracts the elder crowd, the southern side has skateboarding and attracts a much younger crowd. With more than three streets intersecting, the *Place de la Bastille* is one of the very busy intersections in Paris. I remember this vividly as my parents never left my hand while we were crossing the road. As we walked by the side of the *Bastille*, I noticed stories laid out on the paths of the square. Upon inquiry, I learned that these stories indicated where the original castle stood. Stories like these increase the importance of the place and makes you want to know more, doesn't it?

A stone's throw from the *Bastille square* is *Champs de Elysees*. I can easily say that *Champs de Elysees* is one of my favorites. It is one of the most beautiful avenues you will ever see. A stroll on the *les Champs*, as Parisians call it, is home to several luxury brands. Be it *Banana Republic, Levi's, Manoush, MAC, Louis Vuitton, Hugo Boss, Swarovski, Dior Homme, Celine, Gucci, Chanel, Zara, Sephora, Nike*..... just name it. I also spotted the official PSG store that sells all Paris football club's merchandise. My favorite was, of course, *Sephora*. My mother and I went in promising my dad to be out in 60 minutes; however, we all knew that wasn't going to happen! Mom and I came back with many bags after 150 minutes. We were there for so long that the store played a piece of Indian music for us! My father told me that a huge celebratory event was organized in *Champs de Elysees when* France won the FIFA World Cup in 1998.

I also got to see it again on TV when France won again in 2018—watching it on TV again made me relive my Paris trip. This avenue is almost two kilometers in length. It starts at *Place de la Concorde* and extends till *Arc de Triomphe*. We did not just shop for clothes here. We also ate a lot of food! My parents are also foodies, so we had a wonderful time.

Charles de Gaulle - Étoile - Champs-Elysees

We found a Ladurée, known for mouth-watering French macarons. We made it a point to taste it, and I absolutely loved it. The avenue also has many theatres and cinema halls. Our guide told us that on December 31, people gather on the avenue and welcome the next year with all its glory, watching the countdown displayed on the Arc de Triomphe. Sounds exciting! If any of you readers want to plan a trip to Paris, I recommend you choose December. It is also said that the sun sets right in the center of the *Arc de Triomphe* twice a year. So, watch out!

Another highlight is that the avenue is vehicle-free and safe for children. I have read reports that the street will receive a makeover ahead of the 2024 Olympic Games, and I cannot wait to go back and witness it in person. The memories of *Champ de Elysee* at night, the nice breeze, well lit, and street-side cafe still stays with me.

Eiffel Tower with UEFA symbol to celebrate the win at Euro 2016

We walked along the *Seine* and crossed the river onto the city island to see *Norte Dame*, the 850-year-old majestic building. Famed for its glass windows, dramatic spire, and stone carvings, *Notre Dame* looked very familiar to me, and it was then that I recalled that the cathedral was featured as a backdrop in many films across the globe. Be it *Ratatouille*, *The Three Musketeers*, the 1939 classic *The Hunchback of Notre-Dame*, or *Midnight in Paris*. My father and I even recalled some film scenes as we walked through the cathedral.

I was aware that the building took about 200 years to finish from my readings. 200 years! The fact that the cathedral has survived two world wars and several revolutions and witnessed many key international events. It is one of the most prominent examples of gothic architecture with ribbed vault ceilings and pointed arches and has served as a UNESCO World Heritage site. If you are here, you will not miss the massive bell that hangs right above your head. This bell, Emmanuel, I was told, weighed 13 tons. More than just a piece of metal, it looked like a symbol of joy, progress, and happiness. The cathedral was constructed to symbolize Paris' economic, political, and cultural might in France during its original conception and construction.

As we stood in the queue waiting to enter the cathedral, we could not stop but stare at the Seine riverbanks. However, there was another thing that caught my eye. There was a compass-like figure on the ground. As I had not seen it anywhere else, I was curious. On enquiring, I learned that the compass-like-looking figure was the official reference point representing Paris. Called *point zéro des routes de France* (Point Zero of French Roads), this symbol indicates where all distances to and from Paris are measured from. Although I do not know many details, our guide told us that the dimensions were approximately at a 1:1.61 ratio. I got curious, and when I did some research on this ratio, I learned that this dimension marks perfection in art. The Parthenon in Athens and our own Taj Mahal in Agra were built using this ratio. How cool is that!

I am grateful for having gotten a chance to explore the cathedral in its entirety before the April 2019 fire incident, which destroyed most of the building's roof. Prior to this, the cathedral had also suffered major damage during the French Revolution. I recall newspaper reports and TV news bulletins on how many French and non-French people gathered outside the cathedral and wept, looking at the fire consuming the building. I also remember reading how several churches around Paris rang their bells in response to the blaze. It is said that the renovation of the cathedral will be completed by 2024, before the Olympic Games. Well, let's hope for the best.

I am a great fan of cold brew and generally avoid a cappuccino. However, a cappuccino and croissant on the side of *Notre Dame* stood out for what Paris truly is – a remarkable city, lovely architecture, excellent weather in early summers, refreshing breeze, and great coffee and patisserie. French have their own cooking techniques (flambeing, braising, poaching, and sautéing), and I have noticed that they emphasize baking/cooking with fresh ingredients and simple flavors.

No wonder the word 'restaurant' comes from the French language. And, I do not have to tell you about the excellent way they present their dishes.

When you're in the mood for some home cooking, Paris offers a staggering range of restaurants. You'll never run out of options, from street vendors selling tasty takeaway food to cookers with designer dishes and complicated recipes. Its cuisine has been influenced throughout the centuries by the many surrounding cultures of Spain, Italy, Switzerland, Germany, and Belgium.

Paris has always been known for its café crème and hearty espresso, but more recently, it's also emerged as a specialty coffee capital. With local roasters and barista-led shops now in nearly every arrondissement, Paris is officially on the world's specialty coffee map. Their Pâtisseries are worth traveling all the way to France.

Before our next stop, we made it a point to visit a nearby open market. To give you some context, open markets are highly popular in the country, and from what I know, they have been around since the 15th century.

Farmers, bakers, fishermen, and other enthusiasts come from all over France and participate in this wonderful tradition. If you want to experience the real French-ness, visit an open market. As we were near Notre Dame, my family and I visited the nearby *Maubert Market*. Although we just had a cup of coffee, the market also had beautiful jewelry and scarves.

Your trip to Paris must include *Louvre Museum* on the list. It's one of the world's greatest museums, and it's right in the middle of the city. Situated by the side of *the Seine* River, the museum is spread over a large area of land.

Exhibits at the Louvre

When I say large, I mean it. It entertains about nine million visitors annually and houses over 35,000 pieces of art. If you ask me, you just can't tour the entire museum in one day. Our guide was fantastic, and we were told about the important paintings from many different eras. The 13-year-old me was taken aback by the unique architecture of the museum; the glass pyramid at the beginning, through which people enter the museum, was the highlight for me.

When you think of the *Louvre*, you are likely to imagine one of the museum's paintings, such as *The Raft of the Medusa, The Wedding at Cana, The Mona Lisa, The Venus de Milo, The Coronation of Napoleon* or *The Horse Tamers*. These paintings are often featured in movies. But the Louvre actually contains a vast collection of artifacts from all periods of history. Our fantastic guide walked us through every minute fact about the museum. Following the Renaissance and French Classical style, this museum, I was told, has been an inspiration to many buildings, including the U.S. Capitol in Washington, D.C., and the Metropolitan Museum in New York.

Walking is a wonderful way to get around and explore Paris. This was especially true when we visited in the month of June, as the weather was quite pleasant. The Parisian streets are pedestrian-friendly, so we decided to walk to all our destinations. It was a great decision as the Bollywood songs Ilahi and Cutie Pie echoed in my mind as I recognized the sights from the songs as I walked around the city. I admired the cobblestone lanes and the tall buildings.

Paris' history is interesting. Did you know that metro opened in Paris in the 1990s? Back then, the metro provided a modern, economical way to connect people and places in the large cities of France. Today, the Paris metro is increasingly seen as essential for public transportation. In fact, their system is so good that it was awarded the title of Best Transpiration System 2021. Each Metro stop in Paris has a historical theme, such as architecture, fashion, food, or art. This theme is prominently displayed on the station's exterior.

The hotel we stayed at was not far from *Arc De Triomphe*, an iconic symbol of French national identity. As I strolled admiring the monument, I was informed that this place paid respect to those who sacrificed their lives during the French Revolutionary and Napoleonic Wars. I also noticed all the heros' names inscribed on the monument's outer and inner surface.

As our guide enlightened us with many more stories, I instantly developed great respect for the Arc. It is unfortunate what happened in late 2018 when the monument suffered acts of vandalism as part of the Yellow vests movement protests. I consider myself lucky to have visited this beautiful monument before the il-fated incident.

Up next, we visited the famous Galeries Lafayette. I was looking forward to this visit as Galeries Lafayette is famed as one of the oldest department stores in Paris. If you like walking just like me, there are several Metro stations near the store.

The Galeries Lafayette has many goods, including fashion items, furniture, decorative items, gifts, and food. When you think of a department store, you can imagine a large, modern building with bright lights and huge windows. But that is not always the case. The Galeries Lafayette is a rare surviving example of a 19th-century castellated department store; the architecture will make heads turn. Being the fashionistas we were, my mother and I could not contain our excitement when we spotted brands like Chanel, Dior, Saint Laurent, Chopard, Louis Vuitton, Zara, Topshop, Caroll, Massimo Dutti, Sessùn, Sinequnone, and oh, many many more. I remember how difficult it was for my mother and me to stop ourselves and max out my father's credit cards! Oh, before I forget, if you are someone looking for a career in fashion or just a fashion enthusiast, I highly recommend going to *the Pret A Porter* fair. It is a major International Womenswear Fashion Trade Exhibition. With the unique display of classic to contemporary designs, this fair enjoys a worldwide appreciation and has completed its 100 years. This grand fashion event gives an insight into future fashion trends. This four-day-long premiere fashion show has truly gone international and stepped into the arena of the fashion world. It is a golden opportunity for everyone to discover their inner designer.

There are several famous cafés, bars, and restaurants located in the store. You'll find plenty of French chocolate, tea, oils, mustards, and spices. If you need some time off the 'luxury' shopping, head to the 7th floor, and witness the 360-degree view of Paris. Just talking about it takes me back to the panoramic view of *the Eiffel Tower, the Montparnasse Tower, Invalides,* and *Opera Garnier.* The staff was also kind and helped us with literally everything we needed. They all spoke English, which made our lives easier. So, whatever age group the visitor may belong to, the store has something for everyone.

Let me tell you about our trip to the iconic Eifel Tower. I was particularly excited for this one; I mean, who would not be. Even if you haven't been to France, you will have heard of this iconic tower.

It is the best example of modern architecture. It is so tall that it surpasses even the famous pyramids of Giza in terms of its iconic status. As a 17-year-old, when I think about it now, the Eifel Tower has become a testament to the strength of engineering and architecture. Well, it's hard to fully understand the Eifel Tower until you see it for yourself.

I will tell you a bit about my experience of going up the tower. As I mentioned at the beginning, my father had managed to get the tickets, so we went all the way up to the top floor. I did start to count the stairs, but I soon lost count, witnessing the beauty of the city from the 1st and 2nd floors.

Yes, I recommend taking the stairs and enjoying the view in its entirety. Once we reached the top floor, no one, including my parents, could calm me down. I could spot every tourist spot there is in Paris from the Eifel Tower.

The top floor is guarded and closed, so my parents were also not scared to let me roam around. I also spotted a considerable football marking the event of the UEFA Euro Finals. The city of Love and lights was decked up for the occasion and matches. I must say, our timing was perfect!

Allee des Cygnes

We also visited the site where Princess Diana died, the *Pont de l'Alma* tunnel. I do not know about you, but to me, The Flame of Liberty looked similar to the Statue of Liberty in New York. You know what, I was right. The sculpture is a replica of the torch held by the statue in New York, and in fact, the structure was a symbol of friendship between France and America. The structure has been around since 1989. Eight years later, when the unfortunate accident killed the beloved Princess just under the square, the sculpture became an unofficial memorial for Diana. I remember Elton John's *Candle in the Wind* ringing in my ears when I stood there. The song makes so much sense!

Twilight in Paris

Paris n'est pas une ville, c'est un pays.
- François 1er
(Paris is not a city, it is a country! And a very beautiful one at that.)

5

GERMANY

"Aus den Steinen, die Dir in den Weg gelegt werden, kannst du etwas Schönes bauen." – Erich Kästner, German poet

Translation: *"From the stones that block your way, you can build something beautiful."*

Germany is a country with a rich history dating back to ancient times. The country is known for its beautiful scenery, its many castles, and its efficient economy. Germany is also known for its strong industrialization. The country has a long history of industrialization, dating back to the early 1800s. Today, Germany is one of the most industrialized countries in the world and its economy is the fourth largest in the world. Germany is home to many world-famous companies, such as BMW, Mercedes-Benz, Siemens, and Volkswagen. The country is also home to a large number of small and medium-sized businesses.

The rise of the German Empire as an industrial powerhouse is one of the most significant events of the nineteenth century. A variety of factors influenced the development of industry in

Germany, including the country's large population, rich natural resources, and strong government support.

The German people had a long tradition of hard work and technological innovation, which laid the foundation for the country's success in the industrial age. The discovery of new sources of energy, such as coal and iron, also played a role in Germany's industrialization.

By the late 1800s, Germany had emerged as a leading manufacturing nation, producing a wide range of products, including textiles, chemicals, and machinery. Since the early 1800s, Germany has been one of the leading industrial nations in the world. The Second Industrial Revolution, which began in the late 19th century, only further solidified its position as an economic powerhouse. A major factor in Germany's success was its strong infrastructure and highly skilled workforce. Another key element was its government's willingness to invest in new industries and technologies. This forward-thinking attitude helped German companies become leaders in a number of industries, including chemicals, automobiles, and machine tools. Today, Germany remains one of the top industrial nations in the world, thanks in large part to its rich history of innovation and commitment to progress.

Germany's rise to an industrial powerhouse was due to a perfect storm of factors. One key factor was the presence of natural resources like coal and iron ore. This meant that the German industry didn't have to rely on imports, which made production cheaper. Additionally, Germany had a highly skilled workforce, thanks to the country's strong education system. This allowed companies to produce high-quality goods that were in demand internationally. Finally, the government implemented policies that were friendly to businesses, such as low taxes and deregulation. These factors all contributed to Germany's rapid industrialization and economic growth in the late 19th and early 20th centuries.

History will let us know that the Romans ruled Germany until the Franks defeated them. The Frankish empire influenced Germany's religious faith. The Franks were evangelicals who attempted to convert as many natives to Christianity as possible. Catholics mostly populated Germany through the Middle Ages, but there were many Protestant Reformations within the church circle. Germany's northern and eastern parts turned to Protestantism, while the north and southern parts stayed Catholic.

By the 19th century, Germany had started establishing itself as a supreme power in Europe by conquering many European countries. Their military might was unmatched. Germany's military expanse and its industrial inclination promoted its desire to dominate the rest of Europe. Parliamentary democracy had evolved when Adolf Hitler was appointed as the Chancellor of Germany in 1933, and the rest is history. Adolf Hitler's totalitarian regime and blitzkrieg tactics ensured that the other countries bowed down to their demands. If not, they were threatened with a declaration of war. Hitler evoked antisemitism in his people, which led to the world's biggest tragedy, the genocide known as The Holocaust. More than 6 million Jews were killed, and even more, were left traumatized for life. However, today it stands as an example of atonement. For example, the holocaust and other German war crimes are not hidden or rewritten in the school curriculum. Students are told these stories to know of their country's grisly past. Some of the roads have names carved onto them. They are not names of any famous German celebrity. They are the names of people who were once numbers in horrific concentration camps. The Germans do this to remember everything so that they do not repeat it again.

The genocide was the end of Hitler's satanic intentions and a beginning of a new era for Germany. It refocused on being the powerhouse of the European economy and still stands by that aim. Germany's main goal is to maintain peaceful relationships with all its neighbors, and it does have quite a few of them. Denmark borders Germany to the north; the Netherlands, Belgium, Luxemburg, and France to the west; Switzerland and Austria to the south; the Czech Republic and Poland to the east. It has created an exceptional public education system and welcomed roughly 320k internationals in 2019 alone. Students are largely drawn to Germany for its academic excellence and its low-cost living compared to its rival countries in the same field, like the US and Canada. The state-funded education allows students to get selected for the best universities with plenty of opportunities at a great cost.

The state-funded education is not the only thing that had me impressed about Germany. Codetermination is a concept found in Germany. It is the concept that gives workers the legal right to elect trade union representatives to the Board of their companies. This right gives them the power to participate in the management of their company and the work culture within. Another stellar example comes in the sports domain. Germany is one of the leading countries when it comes to professional football. Many football clubs across Europe have fallen into severe financial crises or folded after over a hundred years due to financial mismanagement by their owners. However, one country that did not attract such news was Germany. Why? Germany has the 50+1 rule which means the supporters are the majority shareholder with 51% of the shares. It has meant that they have a stake in how the club is run.

Hamburg

It was this Germany that provided me with a breathtaking experience. Some cities in Germany are exceptionally industrial. They are filled with mills and factories, the smoke lining up the sky, and the cacophony of whirring and rattling engines, but it was a blissful delight despite it all. I have had the chance to visit this country twice. Once I was a young girl and I can still vividly recall my impressions, after looking at the photographs, as if it happened yesterday. The second time I was fortunate to go on a trip as part of a student exchange program. While these were lengthy trips, I have the chance to be in the country for layovers as Lufthansa is my preferred airline carrier to the West. These planes and the people who staff them are efficient, clean, and precise like their native Germans. If I have to start anywhere, I will start in Frankfurt.

Frankfurt:

Frankfurt, *the ford of Franks* was so named by Charlemagne, the King of the Franks to mark the defeat of the Saxons. It lies around 350 km away from Berlin. Frankfurt has since served as a site for imperial coronations as one of the most significant cities under the Holy Roman Empire. Today, it is incredibly diverse in terms of ethnicity, religion, and culture as many migrants have settled here because of its economic status. Though Frankfurt is most celebrated for its reputation of being the financial capital, the finance and business aspects blur out when compared to the fun and relaxation the city offers.

One such avenue is the multitude of museums available. There is the archaeological museum, which has findings from more than 200,000 years ago. It is thrilling to see physical evidence of such important discoveries. The Museum Giersch of the Goethe University hosts an array of topics ranging from art to science. It also recounts Goethe's footprints across his childhood house: *the Goethe House*. It would be simplistic to just call Goethe a writer and a statesman. His writings form the backbone of German literature. His writings on philosophy have become the bedrock upon which much modern philosophical enquiry and thought have been stimulated. Fascinatingly, he was an editor, poet, and playwright in his free time. His main career saw him practice law. His notable achievements are a source of great pride for Germany and particularly his birthplace, Frankfurt. The Jewish Museum records and remembers the substantial contribution of the Jewish society in Frankfurt. Tens of other museums depict Frankfurt's rich cultural and historical legacy.[11]

However, any conversation about Frankfurt is incomplete without Innenstadt. It is a fascinating place with a rich history and a diverse culture. Situated on the River Main, it is a major financial center and the home of the European Central Bank. With its skyline of tall office buildings, it is a striking contrast to the old city with its medieval churches and half-timbered houses.

Frankfurt's Innenstadt is home to many historical and cultural landmarks, one of the most prominent being the Frankfurt Cathedral. The Frankfurt Cathedral is a Romanesque-style church that was built in the 12th century and has been a key fixture in the city ever since. It is located in the heart of Frankfurt and is one of the most popular tourist destinations in the city. There is also a museum located inside the Cathedral that contains many artifacts from its long history. I was especially awed by seeing the Eschenheimer tower and the Alte Oper.

Frankfurt's population multiplied exponentially by the 14th century. To fulfill the city's growing needs, a proposal was made to expand outside the borders. The emperor was on board with this idea and saw that the 'Second city expansion' was executed. A city gate was built to protect the city from any approaching harm, which is the origin of the famous, Eschenheimer tower. The ground floor of the tower is now a restaurant.

Surprisingly, there is also a subway station right under the foundation of the tower. Once upon a time, that was the only way

---

[11] https://frankfurt.de/english/museums-and-theatres/museums/museums-at-a-glance

to get to the tower. *Alte Oper* translates to the 'Old Opera.' The concert hall was rebuilt in the 1970s after being destroyed by bombs. It has housed salient works of art, including Schreker's *Der ferne Klang* and Carl Orff's *Carmina Burana*.

Frankfurt's Museum District is located in the Innenstadt and is home to some of the city's most popular museums. The area is also home to a number of restaurants, cafes, and shops. Some of the district's most popular attractions include the Museum of Modern Art, the Städel Museum, and the Liebieghaus. Visitors can also explore the historic buildings and monuments in the district, such as the Frankfurt Cathedral and the Römerberg.

Frankfurt's Old Town is a charming area to explore, with its quaint streets and well-preserved buildings. I would recommend starting at the Römer, the ancient city hall which has been standing since the 14th century. Then, wander through the narrow alleys and stop in at the many shops and cafes. Be sure to visit the Kaiserdom, a beautiful cathedral with a fascinating history. For a break from sightseeing, take a walk along the river or explore one of the nearby parks. A good choice would be the Alter Botanischer Garten (Old Botanical Garden).

Innenstadt is one of the most vibrant and lively areas of the city. There is always something going on, and there is a huge variety of shops, restaurants, and cafes to explore. The best way to see everything that the Innenstadt has to offer is to take a walking tour. You can start at the Hauptwache, which is the central square of the district, and then explore the surrounding streets. If you're looking for some shopping, head to Zeil, which is the main shopping street in Frankfurt.

Frankfurt is associated with more than 200 banks, 7000+ enterprises interested in financial services, law firms, consulting agencies, and auditing companies. Furthermore, Frankfurt is also the seat of the European Central Bank. The Frankfurt Stock Exchange is an integral part of its impeccable economy. Frankfurt's reputation scaled up when it incorporated a fully electronic trading system. It also boosted Germany's reputation as a leader in electronic trade systems. Unlike many other cities we have discussed in this book, Frankfurt does not attract many visitors due to its impression of being a more commercial city. But those who visit Frankfurt once will know that the city is underrated as a tourist destination. Frankfurt focuses on finance, transport, and trade fairs to conduct its economy. Frankfurt's airport is the largest in the country. Frankfurt attracts many companies to set up bases in its city due to its superb logistics and infrastructure. Frankfurt is also a focal point of the German motorway network.

Frankfurt has a unique food culture. Germany's food has also been accused of being boring and tasteless. The Germanic tribes consumed barley, wheat, some dairy products, and occasionally, meat. Though, as Germany grew, it adapted techniques from Italians, French, Poles, Turks, and Jews. Every region of Germany has its own specialty. The variation naturally depends on geography. The most surprising thing is the city's market food/street food culture. Despite several existing, well-established, and notable restaurants, I was eager to try the street food. I was delightfully shocked by the varieties.

One of my memorable culinary experiences was having breakfast with my father at Marriot. We had eggs with bacon and the accompanying potatoes and bread were perfect with the right amount of crispiness and fluffiness. He talked of how the ISH fair was held at the adjacent Trade Fair Ground. My father had been a part of this fair many times. My father told me that it would take close to four days and over 25000 steps to visit every nook and cranny of the fair. He spoke of the various food stalls which sold German specialties including sausages.

On my culinary exploration, I came to realize that sausages were the most preferred snacks, reflecting the general Frankfurt obsession with this snack. I remember stopping at a butchery stall and could notstanz help but marvel at the unending varieties of sausages that were stocked. These sausages are prepared on open pans. Other dishes included steak and fries, rotisserie chicken, salads, and even Chinese bowls.

There is a market hall in Kleinmarkthalle, where most grocery stores double up as eateries. Most customers eat outdoors. I tried one of the preferred local delicacies, Frankfurt hard-boiled eggs and crown cake served with green sauce. The green sauce is a blend of seven herbs: borage, chervil, cress, parsley, salad burnet, sorrel, and chives. If there was ever an appetizing green sauce, it was here that I found it.

Stuttgart and Esslingen:

Stuttgart is a two-hour drive from Frankfurt. The two cities are not entirely dissimilar. However, the destinations and the architecture in this city were few and far less captivating than in Frankfurt. Stuttgart, like Frankfurt, is an industrial city. It is famous for its automotive industry. I also had the chance to visit Esslingen, a small town in the Stuttgart region. I was fortunate to land an opportunity to stay in a German home for ten days. The idea was to truly experience the German lifestyle. Every traveler dreams of experiencing a place in its truest form. What does a city look like when it is not on display? How does it function when it is not aiming to captivate the eye of a tourist? What is it like to live like a local and experience a city like it were my own?

All these questions were answered during my 10-day stay in Stuttgart. I remember standing in front of Gate No 6 at Indira Gandhi International Airport and feeling mixed emotions. I was nervous, overwhelmed, and excited all at once. Well, it's not like I have never been to the country before. But I was excited to explore a country that I kind of knew but was at the same time foreign to me. This trip was not for leisure, though, but rather a chance for me to explore my third language, German, and put it to the test. I was part of an exchange program organized by my school. We were supposed to go to Germany and immerse ourselves in the culture and language for the next 11 days. We had a morning flight to Istanbul from where we were supposed to connect to Stuttgart. The airplane ride was fun, and I had a blast at the Istanbul airport.

Although I was traveling with my teachers, seniors, and classmates, it felt different; I felt more independent, responsible, and conscious of my surroundings. It was going to be an exciting trip as I would be meeting Sandra who had stayed with me during the previous Diwali as part of the program. She and her school did not disappoint. Her schoolmates had shirts made which featured the logos of our schools. We were touched by their warm gesture.

It was lovely to meet her parents and the first impression I had was they were very tall. But the long hours spent traveling had a cost and I ended up with a high fever. Sandra's mother, Mrs. Vukic, was sweet and gave me the proper medications, which helped me sleep through the night. The next day I had a quick call with my parents who scolded me for not calling them when I had reached Stuttgart. I was still not back to full health and I was diagnosed with stomach flu. It could have been due to the airplane food. However, I felt better when we went around the city like a little treasure hunt of finding places, munching fresh strawberries along the way.

Sandra and I joined my friend Avani and her exchange partner Felipe to tour the city separately. It massively helped that the four of us had become good friends and we were able to fully enjoy the city. We went up a hill on a train, and the sites were magnificent. We ended the day with a visit to the Fernsehturm.

View from the Fernesehturm

We spent the next day at their school and its Geschwister Scholl gymnasium. We participated in their school classes and activities and also gave the German students a little insight into our school through a video presentation. We also tried their school lunch which featured potato gratin, fritters, and salad. On day three we went to see the Ludwigsburg Castle. I had fun playing with Christina, Sandra's sister. We had a lot of fun by indulging in a lot of train and boat rides. We had Schnitzel and fries and took many pictures. Schnitzel, a dish that originated in Austria, is made by tenderizing a piece of meat (such as chicken, beef, veal, or pork) and then covering it in egg, flour, and breadcrumbs before frying it in oil. It is very similar to a French escalope. This dish is an excellent example of the typical German food served in bars, restaurants, and fast-food eateries.

Schnitzel

Pairing the schnitzel with fries is a trendy and satisfying choice. I spent the next day relaxing at Sandra's house. I wanted them to have an exposure to Indian cuisine and cooked them a sumptuous meal of paranthas, jeera aloo, egg Maggi, and thepla. They did not leave me to my own devices. Sandra's best friend joined her and Mrs. Vukic in the kitchen and made fried chicken and Greek salad. It was a fun-filled experience as we exchanged notes on cooking and had a lovely day.

There were no leftovers but plenty of conversation and jokes. We were full of food and mirth. Then Mrs. Vukic, a hairstylist by profession, gave us a little makeover by washing our hair, styling it, and doing our nails. The next day we spent souvenir shopping and trying other delicacies. I loved the Käsespätzle which is a dish from the southwestern regions of Germany. It is made from layering small Spätzle pasta with grated cheese and topping with fried onion. It is usually served with a salad and sometimes with applesauce. It was salty but the condiments served really complimented the dish making it a wonderful dish. We then visited another German exchange student, Amelia at her house for an evening barbeque. Amelia was the exchange partner of my senior Saumya. Saumya had also invited her classmate Chhavi and her exchange partner to the barbeque. It was another fun-filled session as we made fresh bread and cooked it by the fire. The dining experience was elevated by the divine garlic butter made by Amelia's mother. We paired them with grilled chicken and pork sausages.

Barbecue with my hosts

The next day, Mrs. Vukic took me to Esslingen am Neckar along with her best friend and her beautiful puppy. She is one of the most knowledgeable people I have ever met, and we had a lot of fun with her. We had gelato and soaked in all the little town vibes. We also visited her castle-like home which was beautiful. In the evening, Sandra's grandmother made tri-color pasta with fresh homemade tomato soup which we topped with Parmesan cheese. To this day, it is one of the best dishes I have ever had. It was so good that we ate the leftovers for the next two days. The seventh day of the trip was spent at Konstanz where we saw the beautiful Lake Constance.

 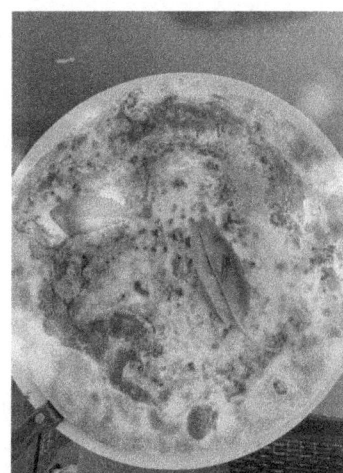

The delights at Konstanz

I also have fond memories of this place as I had my first pizza of the trip here and it turned out to be the second-best pizza I have ever had at the time of writing. The next day we took a road trip to visit the Neuschwanstein castle. It was a picturesque and scenic drive making the journey equally impressive as the destination. Upon returning, we had Kartoffelpuffer. This dish is similar to a swiss 'Rosti': a shallow fried pancake made from grated potatoes, egg, and flour. It is sometimes eaten with eggs and bacon for breakfast in Germany, or as a side with meat for lunch or dinner, or on its own with applesauce.

The next day, I witnessed German engineering firsthand when we visited the Mercedes Benz Museum and the Mercedes Benz Untertukheim Plant! Fortunately, no prior reservations were required for the tour. During the tour, I ordered a replica of the Mercedes classic 300SL for my father as it has been his dream to own that Mercedes car. I also bought it as a promise that I would believe in the future and its infinite possibilities. We also went to a Bretzel-making factory where we learned how to make one of our own bretzels. We were even allowed to take some home. Bretzel is the German term for a pretzel, although you may see them sold under either name.

Available at bakeries and in street stalls, a bretzel is made with a long strip of dough which is folded into a knot and then boiled before being baked. This results in a chewy brown crust and a soft fluffy interior. It is typically flavored with salt, seeds, or cheese and served with a mustard dip. The origin of the Brezel is fiercely contested, but they have long been associated with Christian celebrations, with many viewing the knot shape as a symbol of the holy trinity. We spent the penultimate day at the Ritter Sport Museum where we made our chocolates.

I made myself a hazelnut marshmallow chocolate which tasted and smelt divine. We even got our lab coats and designed the covers of our chocolates. The final day was bittersweet. The days had flown by and it was time to say goodbye to everyone. We gave a cultural dance performance and left the school to go straight to the airport. I was sad that I wouldn't be able to meet Sandra for a long time, but I was very excited to reunite with my parents.

As I left Stuttgart, I could not help but reflect on how the city despite being much smaller than Frankfurt, was so well established. It is spread over many hills in the form of beautiful vineyards. It is surrounded by valleys and parks. The city suffered greatly during the time of war. However, it bounced back just as quickly. By 1952, Stuttgart became a prominent city in terms of economic and industrial features. I was amazed by the automotive tradition that was deeply rooted in this city.

The town of Esslingen caught my attention as I was fascinated by the number of architectural designs in the town. The town has more than 200 half-timbered houses that radiate an unmistakable aura. The town has a long history, dating back to 1300 BC. This stands in great contrast to Frankfurt, which was established in the first century. The archaeological finds trace back to the Neolithic period, indicating Esslingen's early origin.

The city also sheltered around 47,000 refugees affected by the Second World War. To meet the demands for housing, houses in Oberesslingen and Zollberg were created. The Altes Rathaus and the Villa Merkel were the most interesting architectural points I visited in this region. The Altes Rathaus is the medieval town hall still partly preserved from the damages caused by WWII. Stuttgart is known to be the origin point of the automotive industry. The automobile and motorcycle were suspected to be invented and industrialized in Stuttgart. The automotive industry is the pillar of Stuttgart's economy. The Mercedes-Benz group, Bosch, Porsche, etc., are headquartered in Stuttgart. There are also several family-run businesses and SMEs connected to electronics and automotive businesses.

It is also a beacon for academic and research organizations. It can be seen from the high density of R&D and educational centers. The Stuttgart Stock Exchange is a powerful add-on, as it is the second-largest Stock Exchange after the Frankfurt Stock Exchange. As I said a moment ago, the hills of Stuttgart are covered in vineyards. Naturally, the Germans began the production and trade of wine. To date, Stuttgart is among the largest wine-producing cities in the world. The locals celebrate the contribution of the wine trade to the region's economy every year at their annual wine festival called Weindorf.

The food traditions in this city were not very different from the scenes in Frankfurt. I particularly enjoyed a dish called Spatzle. It is a flour dumpling meal served with zwiebelrostbraten, which is typically roast beef and onions. I also indulged in a delicious bowl of flädlesuppe, a flavorful soup with soft, long pasta. It was comfort in a bowl. In Esslingen, I visited the Palmscher Bau restaurant. I had their specialty of grilled sausages and roast beef stew (Sauerbraten). My love for sausages doubled in size after this meal, and I don't think there was any better way to end the trip.

6

GREECE

"Unless you have seen the houses of Mykonos, you can't pretend to be an architect. Whatever architecture has to say, it is said here."
— Le Corbusier

Greece lies around 500 miles to the west of Italy, separated by the Ionian Sea. It is the land of legends, gods, grapes, and games. The sea is an important part of this country. Everything in Greece starts and ends with the sea.

In fact, no part of Greece is more than 137kms away from the ocean.[12] The scent of the salty ocean air and freshly sourced seafood will follow you everywhere.

As I stood under the ever-shining Greek sun, I soaked myself in the beauty of this land of lore. As I sat admiring the view, I was reminded of the phrase *Dolce en niente* – the sweetness of doing nothing. The air in Greece has a strong presence. It is as if a god is watching over you all the time. It was Greece that introduced the idea of the Olympics Games.

---

[12] https://www.trafalgar.com/real-word/facts-greece/

While Pierre de Coubertin introduced the modern version today[13], it is suspected that the Olympic Games commenced around 776 BC. However, experts claim that it could have started sooner than that. *Olympia* was a part of Greek tradition thousands of years ago, which inspired the idea of the Olympic Games. The name originates from the word Olympus where the Greek gods resided.

Greece is responsible for many great contributions to the world in western literature, philosophy, and civilization. Socrates, Plato, Aristotle, Hippocrates, and many more have their roots in Greece. Socrates and Plato's ideas still exert great influence in the world. Greece is known as the cradle of democracy when it comes to politics. The world's first-ever democracy was established in Athens.

However, before I talk about the places I visited in Greece, I cannot help but talk about modern Greece and its financial crisis. Greece's financial crisis was caused by a number of factors, including high government spending, high levels of borrowing, and a variety of other structural problems within the Greek economy. These factors led to unsustainable levels of debt, which eventually led to the country's debt crisis.

What certainly did not help was the global financial crisis of 2008. It further contracted Greece's economy sharply. The country's debt burden increased, and its government struggled to finance its operations. In 2010, the Greek government implemented austerity measures in an effort to reduce its deficit. These measures included cuts to public spending and increases in taxes. While the austerity measures helped to reduce the deficit, they also led to a decline in economic activity and an increase in unemployment. In 2012, the Greek government reached an agreement with private creditors to restructure its debt. This agreement helped to ease Greece's financial crisis and paved the way for the country's recovery as it provided Greece with billions of euros in financial assistance. Finally, Greece enacted reforms to improve its economy. These reforms included privatizing state-owned companies and making it easier for

---

[13] https://www.penn.museum/sites/olympics/olympicorigins.shtml

businesses to operate in Greece. Greece's economy has slowly begun to recover in recent years, with GDP growth of 0.9% in 2015 and 1.8% in 2016. Greece is now starting to recover from the crisis. The economy is growing, unemployment is falling, and poverty is declining. Greece still has a long way to go, but the country is on the right track. It has been over a decade since Greece first fell into financial crisis, and the country is still working its way back to stability. In recent years, Greece has made significant progress in repairing its economy and regaining investor confidence. The Greek government has implemented tough austerity measures, reformed its tax code, and reduced its budget deficit. These reforms have helped Greece return to growth and start to repay its enormous debt burden. While Greece's recovery is still ongoing, the country has made significant strides in stabilizing its economy and rebuilding confidence in its future. One of its significant earnings comes from tourism and I was more than happy to contribute as Greece is a place of remarkable culture and history. There is no better place to start than in its capital, Athens.

Athens:

Athens is beautiful in a jaw-dropping, unforgettable way. It features the Acropolis to the Temple of Zeus. It was once the heart of the Neolithic Age's most powerful civilizations. Today, it is dominated by colossal architectural achievements of its past. Athens' modern-day contemporary galleries and laid-back cafes have matched the standard. There have been many popular books and films set within the myths of Greece.

Movies like Clash of the Titans and Three sisters of Fate, and the Percy Jackson books by Rick Riordan allured me into the world of Greek Gods. Athens is named after the Greek goddess of wisdom and war, *Athena*. I took it upon myself to visit Athens, the origin of democracy and the cradle of European culture when I was 16 years old. The Acropolis Museum elegantly glows over Athens as if it were a sun in a box devoted to the Parthenon and its neighboring monuments. The enormous glass windows elegantly blend the old and new sections of the city, creating a dynamic experience. I recommend beginning your tour from the 'Parthenon Gallery' summit and working your way downhill. The museum's literature will also be of great help on this route as it will tell a far more cohesive tale, and you can avoid the problem of rushing through the museum's ultimate highlight – the head of Alexander with its exquisite sculpture work and finesse. It is regarded as one of the best sculptures in the world. An impressive sight is that of the Calf-Bearer. It is a metal sheet depicting Gorgon – a mythical monster with eyes wide open, the Statuette of Athena Promachos, and the gorgeous head of Alexander the Great. I was mesmerized by the stunning views of the monument, including the floor's glass paneling and elevation.

Change of Guard in Athens

However, if you find yourself in Athens, be sure to visit the Parthenon! This incredible temple was built in 447 BC and is a true marvel of ancient architecture. While the Parthenon is currently in ruins, it is still an awe-inspiring sight to behold. Trust me, a visit to the Parthenon is a must-do when in Athens!

I can vouch that the ruins only heighten the allure of the place. The Parthenon is a temple that was built in 447 BC in honor of the goddess Athena. The temple is widely considered to be one of the most important buildings in the history of Western architecture. One of the reasons why the Parthenon is so important is because it was one of the first buildings to be made entirely out of marble. The Parthenon is also significant because it represents the peak of the Greek Classical period. It is one of the most well-preserved examples of ancient Greek architecture. The Parthenon is also a symbol of democracy, as it was the site of the first democratically elected government in Athens.

The city's rich network of taxis and terminals sparked my motivation to explore the *Erechtheion shrine* and ruins. It is a site with a rich history of Greece's ancient engineering. The rocky outcrop of Areopagus was also an exciting feature of the trip. Areopagus was the place where the war god Ares was supposed to have been tried for the murder of Poseidon's son. Though the origin of this place is unknown, it is presumed that it might have served as a council of elders in pre-classical times.

The Athenian economy was mostly based on trade. It experienced a scarcity of food. So, they had to take advantage of their proximity to the sea to trade with other cities and acquire food for their residents. If you visit Greece, the first scent to hit your nose will be olives. Athens is popular for olives and olive oil production. The olive tree also holds great symbolic meaning. An olive branch is known to stand for peace and victory. It is even used as a literary device to convey peace. Once every four years during the Panathenaic Games, the winner could take home about 5 tons of olives. Talk about getting rich overnight!

Due to the high availability and the love of olives, the Greeks cultivated them throughout the country. Eventually, olives were in demand, and thereby, Greeks began to trade them to neighboring countries. Naturally, the winners of the Panathenaic Games were the greatest merchants selling olive oil. We can see how it boosted their economy.

To this day, Greek remains one of the prominent exporters of olive oil globally.[14] Honey is another substantial element that the Greeks love and produce. Even before there was olive oil, there was honey. Athenians traded honey to their neighboring countries. The Greeks were also famed for their painted pottery. This dates back to the stone age. The durability of these vases is exceptional. Archaeologists discovered many pots and pottery shards in excellent tale-telling states. Pottery was used for multiple reasons in Greek culture. There is obvious use in the kitchen and for wine drinking. Large amphoras were made for marking the graves. Finer pottery was exported as a valuable item. As a matter of course, it boosted the economy of Athens.

Athenians imprisoned thousands of slaves. The enslaved people were put to work in the silver mines of Laurium, about 50 km away from Athens. These mines also produced copper and lead, making Athens wealthier by the day. Athenians traded olive oil, honey, silver, and finely painted pottery to Italy and acquired wood and food grains in return. These items were also sold in the marketplace along with other fine items like jewelry, leather sandals, clay oil lamps, etc. The marketplace went by the name *agora*, and it was a massive extravaganza.

Athens' financial growth made it Greek's financial capital. It serves as the headquarters of well-known companies like Hellas Sat, Hellenic Aerospace Industry, Mytilineos Holdings, Titan Cement, Hellenic Petroleum, Papadopoulos E.J, etc. From Sony to Coca-Cola, other multinational companies have also set up R&D bases in Athens. While tourism acts as the preeminent contributor to the city's wealth, the banking sectors, transportation and education provide a parallel income. Culturally, Athens is famous among archaeologists who have set up numerous research centers in the city. The museums in Athens are big attractions for tourists. When it comes to cultural legacy, Greece is second to none. Athens has 148 theatrical stages, the most in the world.

---

[14] https://www.greek-olive-oil.com/history.html

The same energy is shown toward sports in Athens. Greece was the origin of the Olympic games, and it was probably only fair that it got a good number of chances to host it. Athens has hosted the Summer Olympics twice so far. The stadium has the reputation of being one of the most beautiful stadiums in the world. It has also hosted the Euros finals thrice. Many multinational sports clubs call Athens home.

Acropolis

However, the architecture of Athens is different from any other city. You will not see any building looking to pierce the sky. It is partially due to the height restriction imposed by the government. However, while these buildings may not wow you in terms of height, they will knock you back with their sheer beauty. The Greco-Roman, neoclassical, and modern influences can be seen in the architecture of the city. There is no commonality among the buildings; the past and present co-exist happily. Perhaps, that is what makes Athenian architecture so unique in the first place.

Athenian cafes and restaurants are another treat altogether. After we finished the tour of Acropolis, we strolled inside the charming and family-friendly Old Tavern of Psarras in Plaka. It is almost a century old, and it still maintains its charm of being a lovely local restaurant. It was initially opened in 1898. Fresh fish, meat (particularly lamb), and vegetarian alternatives abound in their typical Greek cuisine and will provide you with the flavor of Athens's unique tastes and style.

The Greeks are experts at flecked and charcoal-grilled meats. My favorite meal was *souvlaki*, roasted meat eaten on pita bread with chopped tomatoes and onions and whippings of *tzatziki*. I later learned that *gyros* (roasted meat served alongside a pita) are also popular when served in this manner.

Local free-range lamb is among the most popular dishes at the tavern and other small Greek cafes. I cannot talk of Athens without mentioning the tantalizing *dolmades*. Dolmades are made of herby rice-spiced vine/grape leaves or cabbage boiled in little rolls. Each area of Greece has its own take on dolmades; either they are hollowed out or served in traditional vine leaf packets filled with vegetables cooked in the oven. Interestingly, the filling was usually made with minced pork and long-grained rice, while veggie variations use herbs for rice flavoring, including dill, thyme, oregano, and fennel.

One cannot leave Greece without tasting the authentic *mousakka*. It comprises a fluffy cheese layer topping, creamy béchamel sauce, tomato-cooked minced meat (we got them to innovate), and sautéed aubergines to create an overall baked exterior. Vegetarians can also opt for the traditional Greek salad with Kalamata Olives and feta which gives it a unique zingy flavor and keeps you cool in the sapping summer.

Athens has many reputed local restaurants, including the fantastic and stylish 360° Cocktail Bar – Monastiraki. It serves Greek meze and outstanding cocktails. Though I had earlier explored the Old Tavern of Psarras in Plaka, this location provides a more relaxed dining experience as it overlooks the ancient center.

If you are an avid shopper and cannot help but buy cotton or linen garments, I will highly recommend the Avisinyas square. If you are a North Indian with the flair for finding a bargain, this place will feel like home. It is not just because of your skill. The place can feel similar to mini Janpath in Delhi. There are many bargain shops, open-air restaurants, and cafes. When we reached Greece, there was another similarity we found to Indian summers. The weather was hot and humid.

We realized that we did not pack enough clothes. Thus my mother and I dragged my father to Avisinyas square to find many wonderful clothes at bargain prices. If you were to ask me, our lack of knowledge of the weather turned out to be a blessing in disguise. About an hour's car ride away from Athens is Sounion. It is a small town in Attica, Greece. Sounion is the best place to explore ancient Greece.

It is located on the southernmost tip of Attica and is home to the Temple of Poseidon. The first thing that you will notice when you arrive at Sounion is the stunning views. The Aegean Sea is a beautiful blue and the coastline is dotted with white buildings. The second thing you will notice is the history. Sounion is the site of the Temple of Poseidon, which was built in the 5th century BC. The temple is an excellent example of Greek architecture and is definitely worth a visit. The temple is located on a headland that juts out into the Aegean Sea, and it offers stunning views of the water and the nearby islands.

It is one of the most well-preserved temples from that era. The views from the temple are incredible, and you can see for miles. There is also a small museum on-site that houses some of the artifacts found during excavations. However, I have a word of caution. The climb to the temple can be exhausting. We did it when the sun was beating down on us at about 38°C and at about 95% humidity.

We were almost wiped out by the time we reached the temple. However, the adrenaline of the historic site saw us through the entire excursion. However, when the tour was over, we had nothing left. So we went to the beach and just laid down under a shade as we let the Mediterranean breeze soothe us into sleep.

Sounion is also a great place to enjoy the beach. There are many small, secluded beaches where you can relax and enjoy the Mediterranean sun. If you are looking for a more active beach experience, there are also some great spots for swimming, snorkeling, and windsurfing.

If you're looking for another amazing place to visit, I would highly recommend the Corinth Canal. It's an incredible feat of engineering and it's definitely worth a visit and is about a day's trip away from Athens. The canal is about 6 miles long and was built in the early 19th century. It is a man-made waterway that connects the Gulf of Corinth with the Saronic Gulf. It is located in the Peloponnese region of southern Greece. The canal is 6.4 kilometers long and 8.3 meters wide. It was completed in 1893 and is one of the most popular tourist attractions in Greece today. The Corinth Canal is a hidden gem in Greece that is definitely worth a visit. It's a great place to take a boat ride, go for a swim, or just relax and enjoy the scenery. The canal is also a great place to learn about Greek history and culture.

Corinth Canal

Santorini:

A trip to Greece doesn't end with Athens, and a trip to Greece isn't complete without visiting its two most popular places: Santorini and Mykonos. My journey began in Santorini. I had booked my stay at Hotel Santo Maris Oia. It was a luxurious hotel and the stay was a present for my mother's special day. The hotel's inviting theme statement was *"Let go and leave everything up to us from this moment on."* I must say that the statement was quickly justified by its eclectic flavors and laid-back elegance that gave visitors an impeccable feel of Greek gastronomy.

Santo Maris Oia offered a spectacular sunset view over the Aegean Sea from the private luxury suite. There is a lot to explore in Santorini's capital, Firá (Thíra) – blue-domed churches, tiny squares, winding lanes, whitewashed terraces, and cubic houses. The houses were painted in white to keep the interiors cool as Greece receives thousands of hours of sun every year, making it one of the sunniest places on Earth.

The incomparable beauty of Santorini prompted a further exploration of the island's prominent attractions like the Santorini Cable Car in Fira, Theresia Island, Prophet Elias Monastery, and Santorini Volcano and Hot Springs and Red beach. I even had the chance to fulfill my sunset wishes of witnessing one at the Kamari Open Air Cinema with a relaxing juice.

Santorini is known for its stunning white-sand beaches, dramatic cliffs, and crystal-clear waters. There are avenues to enjoy many different activities such as hiking, swimming, and exploring the island. There are also many different attractions to see such as the ruins of the ancient city of Thera, the volcano, and the Black Sand Beach.

I was left stunned when I saw the Caldera! It's massive and so beautiful. The volcano is another of the most popular tourist destinations in Santorini.

The volcano is located in the center of the island and is visible from almost anywhere on the island. The volcano has been active for thousands of years and is still active today. The last major eruption of the volcano occurred in 1950 and was one of the largest eruptions in recorded history. The eruption caused massive damage to the island and killed over 100 people. The volcano is now a popular tourist destination and has a number of restaurants, hotels, and shops located near it.

I was also amazed when we took the chance to check out the hot springs. The springs are located in a small village called Thermisia and are easily accessible by bus or car. The water is said to have therapeutic properties and is a popular spot for locals and tourists alike. There are several pools to choose from, each with different temperatures, so you can find the perfect one for you. Be sure to bring your camera, as the views from the springs are breathtaking.

I was also amazed by the ancient sites of the Akrotiri Archaeological Site and the Ancient Thera. The Akrotiri Archaeological Site is a well-preserved ancient city that was destroyed by a volcanic eruption in the 17th century BC. The site includes houses, temples, and other buildings that give insight into the lives of the ancient people who lived there. The Ancient Thera on the top of a mountain is another well-preserved ancient city that was also destroyed by a volcanic eruption. The site includes a theater, an agora, and other public buildings that offer a glimpse into the lives of the ancient Greeks. The climb may seem intimidating. However, I can assure you that it is well worth your while. If you are not as taken by the ancient structures, the mountain also provides the stunning view of the Aegean Sea.

My stay at Santorini was illuminating as I learned about its history. It is said that thousands of years ago, Santorini- then known as *strongili*, fell victim to one of the strongest volcanic eruptions. It is suspected that this eruption caused a tsunami that erased the Minoan civilization off the shores of Crete.

The tsunami is also the origin of the myth, 'The legend of Atlantis.' There is not much evidence on the topic, but there are many theories that can make one visit Santorini. Santorini is the only caldera that is inhabited.

Santorini

On the brighter side, the volcanic ash soil enriches the agriculture sector of Santorini, producing some of the finest cherry tomatoes and other produce in the world. The island also produces wine from an impressive variety of grapes called the *Assyrtiko grape*. Visitors can see the end-to-end experience of winemaking. The agriculture and wine industries add a significant bonus value to Santorini's economy, but the tourism industry is its biggest pillar.

I also ventured to extend my palate in Santorini. I remember having octopus for the first time at a shanty near Ammoudi Bay. The catch was fresh. I remember the heat as sweat poured down with the sun's heat. I could never have imagined it before. My vegetarian friend cringed at the idea of having an octopus. I was told it could be slimy and could disgust me.

However, it was extremely delicious and I smiled at her only to see her busy with her fries and coke. After a week of such experimentation, we finally found ourselves at the Jaipur Palace Hotel to have some Indian dishes at last.

Santorini is famous for delicious Greek food such as the *saganaki*, an addictive dish defined by frying cheese and drizzling honey over a covering of filo pastry. Interestingly, the local chefs informed me of the irresistible taste of saganaki sourced from its gooey, warm, and crispy cheese during preparation. Another fantastic food authentic to the Island was *chlorotyri*, a slice of palatable goat cheese with a creamy but sour taste. It was fascinating that local producers only produce goat cheese in small quantities to maintain its uniqueness to the people. *Fava* is an iconic traditional food in Santorini containing a yellow split peas puree. The comforting dish was my favorite due to its creaminess and simplicity, which has passed on for centuries. While enjoying these meals, I also learned that locals frequented a restaurant called the *Nikolas Oinomagiremata* in Fira, the oldest eatery.

The old-style Aegean taverns decorations, preserving atmosphere, and cuisines like tomato fritters and local fava made Santorini an unforgettable place.

Mykonos*:*

If Santorini is for sunsets, Mykonos is for party and buzz. We went to Mykonos on a cruise liner which took approximately 2.5 hours. It is the most comfortable way to go although the luggage loading and collecting process could do with a massive improvement. We stayed at Plato's Giolos beach. It is the most famous beach in Mykonos, although my personal favorite was Ornos with its lovely surroundings and the youthful crowd filling taverns.

The highlight of the trip was when we hired a private yacht and did one-day sailing in Mykonos. We felt royalty as we had the boat to ourselves. A private chef served us sumptuous meals. I experimented with mussels for the first time on the yacht. They looked thoroughly unappetizing when they landed on my table. However, looks can be deceiving as they were heavenly to taste and eat. The icing on the cake was when the boat anchored itself in the middle of the ocean. As a family, we took a dive and went swimming in clear turquoise waters with the small fish for company.

Visiting Mykonos is like stepping into a postcard of Greece. The island is drenched in sun, surrounded by azure waters, and features stunning architecture. Mykonos is truly a place where visitors can relax and enjoy Greece's natural beauty. Some of the best beaches in Mykonos are: Paradise Beach, Super Paradise Beach, Agrari Beach, Elia Beach, and Psarou Beach.

All of these beaches have crystal clear water and stunning views. They are perfect for swimming, sunbathing, and relaxing. There are also many beach bars and restaurants, so you can enjoy a refreshing drink or a delicious meal while enjoying the incredible views. Mykonos is also home to many historic sites, such as the 16th-century Windmills of Mykonos, the ancient ruins of Delos, and the picturesque Little Venice.

The windmills of Mykonos are a sight to behold. These beautiful structures have been a part of the island for centuries, and their history is as fascinating as their appearance. The first windmills were built on Mykonos in the 16th century by the Venetians.

They were used to grind wheat and barley, and were an essential part of the island's economy. In the 18th century, the windmills fell into disuse and were abandoned. In the early 20th century, there was a revival of interest in the windmills, and they were restored to their former glory. Today, they are one of the most iconic sights on the island

Delos is an ancient Greek island known as the birthplace of Apollo, the god of the sun. The island was once home to a large and prosperous city, which was destroyed by a massive earthquake in the 2nd century BC. Today, the island is home to a number of ancient ruins, including the Temple of Apollo, the Sanctuary of Dionysus, and the Theatre of Dionysus. The island was once a thriving hub of trade and culture but is now an uninhabited archaeological site. Despite its current state, the ruins of Delos are some of the most well-preserved in the world and provide a glimpse into the past.

The ancient ruins of Delos are located on a small island in the Aegean Sea. The island is uninhabited, but the ruins are some of the most well-preserved in the world. The site includes temples, homes, and public buildings that date back to the height of the city's power in the 4th century BC. To get to the island of Delos, take a ferry from the nearby island of Mykonos. The ride takes about 30 minutes, and once you arrive, there is no need for a guide – the ruins are open to exploration.

Once a thriving commercial center and the birthplace of Apollo, the ancient ruins of Delos now stand as a silent testimony to a long-forgotten civilization. As I explored the ruins of temples and homes, and strolled through the ancient streets, I could not help but imagine what life was like in this once-bustling city.

Mykonos' museums, shops, whitewashed churches, party atmosphere, and beach bars are some of its charms. Mykonos is often called *the island of the winds* due to the strong Meltemi winds; the windmills were an obvious addition to the island.

The settlement is Mykonos' definition of Cycladic architecture. There is a fish market that offers bargain prices for local seafood delights. Kato Myli Windmills were a sight to see from afar. They date back to the 16th century and overlook a place called Little Venice.

Then there is the Panagia Paraportiani Church. It is one of the most photographed whitewashed churches. The number of churches in Mykonos can shock you. It is said that there is at least one church per local family in Mykonos. Mykonos also follows a strict color code.

Residents can only paint their windows and doors in three colors per the code. They are blue, green, or red. This code was established to maintain the authenticity of the island. The story behind these colors is equally fascinating. Long ago, the sailors used to paint their doors in blue color representing the sea. The farmers painted them green representing the crops. Everyone else painted it red. These colors stand out in greater contrast as the walls are whitewashed.[15]

My curiosity was sparked by Little Venice, a waterfront offering a taste of Greek cuisine to the locals. It is also considered the

---

[15]https://kinglikeconcierge.com/facts-about-mykonos

birthplace of Apollo and Artemi. It is quite a romantic spot, and the original name of this place was *alefkandra*. However, it is now known as Little Venice due to its resemblance to Venice in Italy. Mykonos, like Santorini, excels in the tourism department. The island attracts around 2 million tourists every year. It has over 40 beaches and is one of the most LGBT-friendly places globally. However, it wasn't always like this. Mykonos focused on growing grains till the 16th century, which formed a large part of its economy.

Mussels – a must have Greek beach food

I tried local cuisines like the traditional Greek classic moussaka. The creamy flavor of moussaka was incomparable; the addition of thyme and cinnamon served in an infusion of mixed salad, and chunky bread proved to be a delectable concoction. Another stellar dish was the Greek lasagne.

It is more commonly known as pastitsio. It is a baked dish with a spicy blend of ground chicken and pasta. It had a thick layer of cheese sauce and cinnamon-spiked red wine meat sauce. The pasta was made in the tubular bucatini style. I also learned of Mykonos' specialties such as *louza*, made from spiced and thinly sliced pork, the aromatic and local appetizer, *ksinotira*.

It was common for locals to indulge in some of these cuisines in renowned local places like To Kafeneio tou Bakoya. Established in the 1970s, this locality provides local fishermen with sea urchins and a meze of sausages.

My exploration of Mykonos and Santorini was a fraction of what these islands in Greece have to offer. They are, but a peek into a life of legend and love. As I mentioned before, the trip to Greece doesn't end with Athens. Nor does it end with Santorini and Mykonos. The journey to Greece is one that you carry in your heart till you visit it again. And then it repeats. I could not help retrace my unforgettable experiences as I booked my flight back.

7

ITALY

Though airs that breathe of paradise are thine,
Sweet as the Indian, or Arabian gales;
Though fruitful olive and empurpling vine,
Enrich, fair Italy! thy Alpine vales;
Yet far from thee inspiring freedom flies,
To Albion's coast and ever-varying skies!
— Felicia Dorothea Hemans, 'Sonnet to Italy'.

Did I visit Italy? Did I really glimpse at those wondrous alleys laden with history and aroma of culture, the cobblestone streets, and the charming neighborhoods? Sometimes I fail to realize whether my days spent in Italy were a dream! I remember watching 'Eat, Pray, Love'. In "Eat, Pray, Love," Julia Roberts takes us on a fascinating gastronomic adventure, with Italy as the major attraction. You'll see a prosciutto-wrapped melon shown on the screen as it if was framed by Michelangelo on camera. As Roberts eats her Margherita pizza, you can see the legendary L'Antica Pizzeria Da Michele. On the screen, you'll go through Rome's Piazza Navona, the Villa Borghese Gardens, and the lovely Trastevere neighborhood's small cobblestone alleyways. When I stood by those same places, my heart did skip a beat. A city labeled with the grandeur of simplicity. I felt, standing there while watching the crowd, that life in Italy is so simple and sweet. At one point, I felt like staying there forever!

Italy is a boot-shaped peninsula in southern Europe that juts into the Adriatic Sea, Tyrrhenian Sea, Mediterranean Sea, and other bodies of water. Its geographical location has played a significant role in its history. Many of Italy's historic cities, including Rome, are located west of the Apennines in wooded hills. The southern coastlands are hot and dry, with fertile plains growing olives, almonds, and figs. One cannot speak of Italy and its great history without speaking of the Roman empire. Italian art, architecture, and culture blossomed and flourished on a global stage due to the Roman Empire. The two premier artists, Leonardo da Vinci and Michelangelo, were two well-known Italian painters. Italy is also central to the Catholic Church, governed by Vatican City. Rome surrounds it. The sea surrounds Italy, and mountains crisscross its interior, dividing it into regions. The Alps cut across the country's northern regions and are dotted with long, thin glacial lakes. The Apennines mountains run the peninsula's length from the western end of the Alps.

Rome, or Roma in Italian, is a cosmopolitan city of 3.8 million people. It is a cultural city, the capital of Italy, and the seat of the Vatican. It is situated on seven hills along the river Tevere (Tiber). Can you fall in love with a city? If you ask me, I'll say when in Rome you don't have much of a choice!

Stepping into Rome was like stepping into my dreams, it took me a moment to realize I was actually there. As I walked, I felt as If I was walking through the pages of history. All the stories and myths seemed to be so real as if I could see the incidents happening right in front of my eyes.

I had a pizza slice in a snack bar before exploring the city. There are many of these small eateries in Rome where you can eat a sandwich, a slice of pizza, and occasionally spaghetti, either eat in or take out.

And all for a couple of euros. I first noticed the large fountain on Piazza della Republica. When the fountain was unveiled in 1901, the four naked nymphs caused quite a stir. Each of the nymphs is supported by a water animal: a seahorse, a sea snake, a swan, and a strange frill-necked lizard. While watching at the fountains I was humming:

> Three coins in the fountain
> Each one seeking happiness
> Thrown by three hopeful lovers
> Which one will the fountain bless?

"Three Coins In The Fountain," from the film of the same name, is a Frank Sinatra classic. Consider all the individuals who poured their aspirations, goals, and tales into modest five-cent coins as you explore the Roman fountains.

Trevi Fountain, Rome

A word of caution: Because of the heavy heat and sun in the area, staying fit requires staying hydrated. No vacation to Italy is complete without mentioning limoncello drinks; though they do contain alcohol, I had a special one created for me without it.

When we visited the Colosseum and Arch of Constantine, we were reminded of the past: The senate and people of Rome erected Constantine's Triumphal Arch in AD 315 to commemorate Constantine's victory over Maxentius in 312. However, the rich Roman history has been impacted by modernization. Rome has grown rapidly in size since it became Italy's capital in 1870. This has caused issues due to the abundance of archaeological sites. Rome has to be careful undertaking any infrastructure projects. For instance, try digging a subway tunnel when there are valuable archaeological finds all around.

The Colosseum was my next stop. The Colosseo Metro station is located just in front of the monument. As I reached my eyes were overwhelmed with one massive building! I couldn't have asked for anything better. The Colosseum is located in the heart of Rome. It is a large stone amphitheater that was commissioned by the Emperor Vespasian of the Flavian dynasty in AD 70-72 and took ten years to finish. It was known as the Flavian Amphitheater during its heyday for the 'Blood games' that were held here with people and animals.

The Colosseum

As soon as we entered the structure, I began to imagine triumph, glory, and horrors all at once. It was as though I could hear the cries; my eyes saw the blood and gore, and my heart felt the agony of those who were once chained here. The Dungeons were telling a lot of stories at the same time. This massive edifice could accommodate over 50,000 people.

The entire structure was clad in elegant Travertino marble. That was the allure! This was erected by Vespasian in 72 AD and opened in 80 AD, with the funds coming from the booty gained from the Jewish conflict. With a height of 157 feet and a circumference of 1788 feet, it was a superstructure for the time. It comfortably accommodates a football field, with a surface size of 620ft x 513ft and a central arena of 287ft x 180ft. It could house at least 50,000 spectators at any given time, with four stories ranging in height from 34 to 47 feet with each story having 80 arches. The arena floor was 15 feet away from the first row of seats. It was not just a four-story structure, but also included an underground level and tunnels where inmates and animals were kept.

This was in use until the 6th century CE, after which it fell out of favor. It was later damaged by earthquakes and was mined for various purposes. However, on the other side of the road, the remnants of its outermost wall can still be seen!

The Arch of Constantine was only a few feet away. It was constructed at around 315CE. Constantine's victory at the Battle of Milvian Bridge prompted the construction of this structure. Despite its immensity, which measures 21 meters in height and 25 meters in breadth, the Colosseum consumes it.

In the upper half of the arch, there is a large inscription commemorating his triumph. There are ten medallions, eight of which were originally from the Hadrian Monument, which dates from the first and second centuries CE and no longer exists. On the highest panel, there are eight human sculptures and six reliefs. Friezes may be found below the medallion. Panels can also be found on the arches' walls. The Arch of Constantine is one of Rome's most popular tourist attractions. This triumphal arch is located close to

Palatine Hill and the Colosseum. The arch was built following Constantine I's victory over Maxentius in the Battle of Milvian Bridge. This arch's architecture stood in stark contrast to the common forms of architecture seen at the time. Several motifs from other imperial monuments dating back to the 2nd century were used, and this structure was also one of the first to use a special construction style. In the middle of the twelfth century, the monument was incorporated into the Frangipane stronghold. Throughout the sixteenth century, it was restored and examined, but the major effort in this respect occurred in and around 1733 when many lost portions were replaced. The three arches are adorned with relief-carved marble slabs.

During Constantine's reign, it was designed and built as a whole, with materials mostly plucked from previous imperial structures. Despite the clear thematic coherence shown by scene selection, the compositional structure may be separated into various historical and stylistic portions. On the major faces and short side of the arch, reliefs from the reigns of Trajan, Hadrian, and Marcus Aurelius can be discovered, while those from Constantine's reign can be found on the lower half. By juxtaposing distinct events in the Empire's history, they alternate in symmetrical patterns. They offer an excellent example of imperial propaganda's metaphorical language: "a succinct survey of more than two centuries of official Roman art history."

Visiting Rome was a stimulating experience not only because it is one of the world's most architecturally rich cities, but also because there is something very appealing about the city, its legacy, and culture, that caressed and embraced me to experience and explore the realms of history.

While Roman mythology claims that Rome was founded in 753 BC, the site has been inhabited for far longer, making it one of Europe's oldest continually populated places. With a nearly two-thousand-year history, the city that has seen it all, from development to devastation, is still standing strong.

The Vatican City was my next trip. A country within a metropolis!

When looking at the skyline, it appears as if the city has been frozen in time, with every structure so perfectly maintained; it's as if you've stepped into the medieval age, where Michelangelo chiseled stone, Bernini cast a spell on marble, and Da Vinci painted his revolutionary thoughts. The Basilica of Saint Peter is one of the most tranquil places I've ever visited. There are severe clothing regulations when entering Christianity's holiest shrine. One must remember that, if your knees or shoulders are showing, you are not permitted to enter the Vatican (so no off-shoulder dresses or shorts). The sight of Swiss Guards, who are famed for their brutality and gallantry, was also noteworthy. St. Peter's Basilica, the Vatican Museums, and, of course, the Sistine Chapel make up Vatican City, commonly known as the "Holy See".

The Vatican

The Vatican's St. Peter's Basilica has been the centerpiece of the Vatican over the ages, with the number of Christian pilgrims expanding exponentially in the last several decades. The Church is considered to be one of the holiest and biggest churches in the world. The Chruch's finely designed architecture goes back to the 16th century when Italian architect Carlo Maderno completed the previously stalled project. Each statue that makes up the church's front has a spiritual tale to tell.

When you enter the church, you'll see that it's not just one of the world's largest cathedrals, but also a great museum. The church is adorned with works of art by Renaissance masters such as Michelangelo and Bernini. The Sistine Chapel, located about 1 km from St. Peter Basilica, is a visual delight for art aficionados. Originally known as Cappella Magna, it serves as the Pope's formal home and the location where the College of Cardinals elects the next Pope.

The chapel's ceiling is said to be one of Michelangelo's greatest works; it shows the full path of humanity in a sequence of nine paintings, from creation to downfall. It is a must-see location because of the vivid articulation of numerous tales from Catholic history, including the second coming of Christ on judgment day.

The Vatican Gardens are home to 13 museums and 54 art galleries, so if you're planning a comprehensive tour, visit all of them.

It is said that the Vatican Garden began as a tiny gallery for sculpture collections and grew into a 7-kilometer-long complex containing the finest collections of art from many ages and empires. Currently, the museum has a little over 20,000 paintings on exhibit, although it is estimated that the institution has around 70,000 paintings. Vatican City is a small town/country in Rome ruled by the Pope. It has a palace, gardens, and museums that provide tourists with a wealth of knowledge due to its extensive collections from the twentieth century.

Every place in history has its origins, and in Rome, it all began in a place called the Roman Forum, which has been regarded as the city's heart since ancient Rome began. The Pyramid of Cestius was another point of interest. Despite the dilapidation of these buildings, there are some traces of a small fraction of original walls, fallen columns, and triumphal arches visible, drawing people's interest in the origins of ancient Rome.

My experience in Rome is unlike any other European city. The culture is reflected in its architecture. Due to the incalculable immensity of its archaeological and artistic treasures, the charm of its unique traditions, the beauty of its panoramic views, and the majesty of its magnificent villas, Rome is one of the world's most important tourist destinations. You will find numerous museums (including the Musei Capitolini, the Vatican Museums, and the Galleria Borghese), aqueducts, fountains, churches, palaces, historical buildings, and the monuments and ruins of the Roman Forum, and the Catacombs. After London and Paris, Rome is the third most visited city in the EU, with an average of 7-10 million tourists per year, which sometimes doubles during holy years.

Rome is nothing less than a paradise for fashion enthusiasts. The glitter and the glimmer and the stores around me made me go gaga. Although not as important as Milan, Rome is the world's fourth most important fashion center, after Milan, New York City, and Paris. It is ahead of London, according to the 2009 Global Language Monitor. Bulgari, Fendi, Laura Biagiotti, and Brioni are among the few luxury fashion houses and jewelry chains headquartered or founded in the city. Other major brands, including Chanel, Prada, Dolce & Gabbana, Armani, and Versace, have luxury boutiques in Rome, primarily along the prestigious and upscale Via Dei Condotti. Each of these boutiques was dreamlike and I felt transported to a rarefied world of fashion and style. I was equally taken when I saw the Cinecittà Studios. It is the largest film and television production facility in continental Europe and the heart of Italian cinema, where many of today's biggest box office hits are shot. The 99-acre studio complex is 5.6 miles (9 km) from Rome's center and is one of the world's largest production communities, second only to Hollywood, with over 5,000 professionals ranging from period costume makers to period costume makers and visual effects specialists. More than 3,000 productions have taken place here, including The Passion of the Christ, Gangs of New York, HBO's Rome, The Life Aquatic, and Dino De Laurentiis' Decameron. Cinema classics such as Ben-Hur, Cleopatra, and Federico Fellini's films were also made here.

Being in Rome provided opportunities to try new foods and visit local neighborhoods. Cacio E Pepe (cheese and black paper), a snack available at any Roman deli or pizza takeaway shop, and Suppli, another snack available at the same establishments, are two of the city's best local foods.

The most exciting aspect of these foods was the simple ingredients used because they were readily available throughout Rome. They require little energy and are less complicated to prepare. However, there is a sophisticated symphony within that simplicity. There were numerous hotels and restaurants in the area where people could eat. The Osteria Trattoria da Fortunata was the most unique and irresistible place, an ideal spot for locals and tourists, offering the most popular cuisines – Central-Italian, Lazio, Italian, and Romana.

I also had the opportunity to sample the well-known Trecca-Cucina di Mercato, where people can get food cooked seasonally based on the availability of selected ingredients. These places provide various food that focuses on flavors. The aromas of dishes like the spaghetti carbonara and the perfectly cooked cod linger long in my memory. Krishna 13 is not expensive, but the cuisine is excellent. My father felt at ease dipping into conversation with the proprietors since they spoke Punjabi fluently. With the heat in Rome (we traveled in the summer), I never expected to be sipping masala chach in Rome.

When we visited Piazza di Spagna, I couldn't believe I was at one of Rome's most popular tourist destinations. I was giddy with delight as I sat on the famed stairways with the other tourists. The iconic Piazza di Spagna is located at the foot of the Spanish Steps. The Immaculate Conception of Virgin Mary's column is nearby. The Spanish stairs are a majestic 135-step stairway that leads from Piazza di Spagna (the bottom) to Trinita dei Monti, where we could view the church of Trinita dei Monti, which was being reconstructed at the time. Piazza Barberini is actually rather lovely, in my opinion. In the center of the square sits a fountain. Triton, a minor sea god in Roman mythology, is thought to be represented by it. A toast is raised by the sea deity. Four dolphins may be seen below. A very elegant and luxurious Barbary Hotel stands at one end of the area, providing a lovely backdrop for the fountain. A wonderful shop offering Italian pasta and spices is tucked away near Piazza Barbeni. It sells excellent Taralli - my go-to snack during my Italian trip.

Taralli is a toroidal Italian snack popular in the Italian peninsula's southern part. Taralli is a sweet or savory cracker with a texture comparable to a breadstick, pretzel, bublik, Sushki, or baranki. Sugar is sometimes used to glaze the sweet taralli. If you're looking for a gourmet supper in Rome, go to Ristorante Crispi. The restaurant is nestled away in a corner and it serves delicious Italian cuisine. The octopus soup, sea bass, mushroom sauce pasta, and tiramisu are all to die for. I've never had better Italian food. A note to my readers, they don't serve pizza.

There was this fantastic burger joint across the street from our hotel Ambasciatori, and I had a sack full of French fries - my soul food - while my parents ate their burgers, a welcome departure from the Italian cuisine we had been eating the entire journey.

When we visited Milan, I noticed, that Milan has all of the benefits of a major city while being relatively small, making it ideal for a visit because tourists can walk to most of the city's attractions and museums. The Duomo di Milano, an amazing Opera House, a magnificent fortress, old cathedrals, and a wide range of museums and art galleries are among the city's most attractive attractions. Milan is the world's fashion capital. Everyone, even cab drivers, strives to be immaculately dressed.

The Duomo Milano is surrounded by well-known labels, however, if you want to test out an Italian designer, I recommend going to lane 2/3 behind the main area. You'll find some exceptional designer clothes tucked away in corner shops. I bought one such garment, which I subsequently saw Bollywood star Priyanka Chopra wearing during one of her functions.

You could spend days browsing the designer boutiques (and leave your credit card behind as you are so tempted). In India, I typically struggle to find clothes that fit my height; these shops were eye candy, and my parents were eager to let me spend. Some of my favorite outfits and shoes were purchased in Milan from local Italian designers and have proven to be fantastic value for money.

Around the Duomo, there are several open cafes where one may have an espresso with dessert or a meal. We were in the mood for something vegetarian and ordered a basic Burrata salad; the quality of the tomatoes and cheese was exceptional. However, find a restaurant that serves fresh dough and wood-fired pizza in the evenings and you'll understand what a true pizza is; it's like the difference between having idli in a Murugan Idli in Madurai and one from your neighborhood shop.

My overall experience in Milan was like a dream, the shops, and the designs are still freshly embedded in my heart.

My father told me that the train is one of the most convenient and easy methods to get across Italy, but it does not have to be your only mode of transportation. Whether you use the train for all or part of your Italian vacation depends on your schedule. You can easily undertake the traditional Rome-Florence-Venice vacation by rail, and it is the suggested alternative because the train stations in these cities are conveniently placed in the city centers, and you do not need a car to visit them. If you want to go to the countryside or mountains, renting a car is a good idea because it provides you with more freedom and flexibility.

Rome and Venice, two of Italy's most beautiful cities, are only a short train ride apart. The Le Frecce high-speed train is the quickest way to get from Rome to Venice. This modern and luxurious train will whisk you away in 3 hours and 7 minutes. Venice, the capital city of Northern Italy's Veneto and Venezia provinces, is famous for its canals and tourist attractions. I can confidently say that Venice is the prettiest city in the world. Some of the most exciting places I visited were St. Mark's Basilica, San Giorgio Maggiore, and Santa Maria Della Salute, one of the world's most recognized religious temples dating back to the 12th century. Another feature was Piazza San Marco (St. Mark's Square), where most of the city's residents gather for a date, tea, coffee, and mingle with the tourists. When I visited Venice, what attracted me was the Venezian Tour.

St. Mark's Basilica is one of Venice's most popular attractions and a must-see on any traveler's itinerary to Italy! But, with a history dating back to the 9th century A.D., it's also a church with a lot of interesting stories and legends surrounding it. In the 9th century, the first St. Mark's Basilica was built on this site to house very sacred relics—relics that had been stolen! Venetian merchants stole the body of St. Mark the Evangelist, one of the four Apostles, from Alexandria, Egypt, in 828. The gondolas sailing Venice's bustling Grand Canal and lesser canals are one of the world's most recognizable pictures. They are the city on the lagoon's emblem of history, tradition, and romance, and a gondola ride in Venice is one of the most sought-after vacation experiences.

St. Marks Square, Venice

So, when you finally get to Venice and have the opportunity to ride in one of the city's gondolas, you should take advantage of it. Gondola rides are unquestionably romantic and a once-in-a-lifetime event.

While gondolas were formerly the preferred mode of transit for Venetians, particularly the upper classes, vaporetti have since taken over as the primary mode of water transportation in Venice. There were roughly 10,000 gondolas cruising the canals and lagoon a few hundred years ago, but there are just about 400 now.

A gondola is a wooden boat with a flat bottom. It's 11 meters long, weighs 600 kg, and is handcrafted in squeri workshops, of which only a handful remain today. Gondoliers own and operate their own boats, and the trade and profession are frequently passed down from father to son.

We stayed at Hotel Danieli. This five-star Venice waterfront grande dame provides classic luxury and a sense of 14th-century grandeur, as well as a rooftop dining patio with spectacular views of the lagoon. We celebrated my mother's birthday there; the restaurant requires booking 3 months in advance and offers the best sunset view over the canal.

We visited Caffe Florian, Italy's oldest cafe. It is a Piazza San Marco tradition. Since its inception in 1720, it has served a diverse range of dignitaries, nobles, and ordinary people in its magnificently designed and frescoed halls. Gilded mirrors, ancient furnishings, and jacketed waiters add to the opulence. Throughout the year, Piazza

San Marco serves as the focal point of municipal life, hosting concerts, orchestras, celebrations, and formal events. It is alive with activity throughout day and night and should be visited at different times of day to witness how the atmosphere and energy of this enormous location keep up with its visitors and residents. These two locations piqued my interest since they provided information about people's religions and cultural relationships.

Canale della Giudecca, Venice

Furthermore, because the city is known for water and canals, I became curious and interested in visiting Canale Grande (Grand Canal), which sweeps through the heart of Venice and has a major S curve visible from a distance. This waterway connects major landmarks such as Piazza San Marco and the Rialto Bridge.

The city featured tourist-friendly local cuisine, although its main traditional food was fish. Bigoli in salsa, Sarde in Saor, and Baccala' Mantecato were their primary dishes since the locals have a strong passion for preparing fish-based foods due to their plentiful quantity and availability.

Surprisingly, fish is easy to prepare, takes less time, and is served with a preserved sour, sweet, or onion marinade. Similarly, Venice has a plethora of eateries catering to both locals and visitors.

The Trattoria Alla Rampa is the most popular and handy for everyone since it serves favorite foods at a reasonable price that most can afford. Ristorante Dalla Marisa is a locale with reasonable costs where most residents eat and has no menu since they prepare with whatever ingredients are available at the moment. One distinguishing aspect was that these establishments were mostly open during the lunch hour and could serve a large number of customers with as little as they had.

We also took a day trip to Pisa. We took Train Italia and went to Florence and Pisa. Pisa is famous for the leaning tower of Pisa. Another famous sight is the statue of David. David is Florence's most famous work of art, and the city is the heart of Tuscany, known for its wines and brimming with Renaissance influence.

Leaning Tower of Pisa

Blue Grotto, Capri

However, the one-day journey from Rome to Capri Island was my personal favorite. The visit to Capri Island and the trek through the Blue Grotto are truly awe-inspiring. According to legend, nymphs and fairies used to bathe here. It is impossible to put pen to paper and write about the blue grotto adventure.

You require a calm sea and are placed in a canoe where you must bend flat to access a mesmerizing blue grotto. We spent the day on the island of Capri. Capri is an island off Naples.

Capri also includes an upscale Italian shoe store where you can have your size monogrammed and fitted; my mother and I purchased gorgeous sandals there. I also had the limoncello drink specially made for me without the alcohol. I was just doing what the Napolitano do as the limoncello is at the heart of day drinking in Naples. The architectural journey came to a close with a pledge to return.

The finest thing I observed about Italy was how effectively they had conserved their art and culture while embracing modernity, keeping their legacy intact. The cities of Italy are more than simply tourist cities with tremendous architectural and artistic attractiveness. They are cities with heart. Rome is the eternal city brimming with so much history of a long forgone time and the mecca for fashionistas. It can be easy to dismiss Naples as a port city. It does not have the glamorous or scenic as Florence, but it is a place that beats to the local Italian culture. It is also the ideal springboard to the nearby island getaways. Capri can be a showstopper when it comes to natural beauty and shopping. Milan is the beating heart of Italy with its business-centric outlook. It has beauty but it is married to steel. It is also undeniably Italian with the same vibe even though it may not be as highly rated as a tourist destination like Rome, Florence, or Venice.

If Milan can be the business heart of Italy, Florence can be considered the cultural heart of the country. Even though this city can be a tourist hotspot, you will be amazed by its pace of life. It feels more like a small town with streets to stroll through and find hidden delights at some corner. It is the place to take a Vespa bike and immerse in the natural beauty of the cypress trees and the warm Italian sunshine. You may be surprised when I say that the best Italian sunsets can be seen in Pisa. There can be a misconception that this city only has the Leaning Tower to see. But the city is a college town with its legacy including that of being Galileo's hometown. The sunsets with the river flanked by stunning buildings and palaces will make it one of the enduring sights of one's youth. However, Venice is sublime when it comes to the Italian experience. It is not just the canals and the gondolas. It is a survivor when it was a naval base during the Napoleanic and World Wars. It is also a pioneer as it is a city built on water. It is also romantic because the city was still built with such grace and beauty without fear of the water on which it was built. I think that is what I will remember about Italy. It is a country of culture with each city being a bastion of beauty and history.

8

NORWAY

"Pretty didn't do it justice. I felt like we'd sailed into a world meant for much larger beings, a place where gods and monsters roamed freely."
— Rick Riordan, The Ship of the Dead

We were finally in the land of the breathtaking Fjords, lakes, and starry skies. Norway is the destination of choice for significant numbers of people each year. Norway is known as the land of the midnight sun. A place where the sun simply never sets. Yes, it is true. Northern Norway experiences sunlight throughout the 24 hours of a day during the summer months. People have described that this phenomenon, which occurs in June each year, feels like watching an action replay. Norway is also known for its language, Vikings, and sustainable living. The oldest language in the country, Norwegian is also one of the easiest to learn. With its alphabetical script and simple words, anyone can master the tongue with a little determination. Though the traditional perception of Vikings is that they are ax-murderers, they have made significant contributions to the building of numerous civilizations.

Norway experienced a surge in sophisticated institutions throughout the Viking Age. Till the 9th century, Norway was comprised of tiny kingdoms and individual properties.

Norway – a land of Fjords

It is estimated that around nine little domains inhabited much of the Viking land. The Vikings always settled in coastal areas as they relied on the sea. Norway was a sacred place and a trade center for the Vikings. However, they had to leave because there was a lack of farming space. Vikings bought Christianity to Norway, though one can never be sure if they were actual believers.

Nevertheless, the Vikings oversaw the spread of Christianity in Norway. Oslo, the capital of Norway, is home to most of the country's tourist attractions. We reached Oslo by flight. We took a taxi to our hotel. We had a lot of luggage and wanted to take a taxi. However, we had heard the sustainable living in Norway. Before I broach that topic, I would like to take a small detour as I remember an interesting experience with taxis in Norway. We booked an Uber, and we were shocked to see that an S class/E class Mercedes came to pick us up. This is a rare luxury back home.

However, the prices can also be fairly steep. Our fare to the hotel set us back around 200 euros. When we remarked about the price, we were informed by our hotel concierge that most people in Norway take trains. These choices are part of Norwegian measures to reduce emissions and dependence on exhaustible fuel sources. It was my experience of a country where its citizens made such conscious choices. It can be easy to think that they may be forced, but the city ranks among the best in happiness indicators. When in Norway, we did as the Norwegians and took a train ride ourselves. We were impressed by the seating and luggage section in these trains. They were indeed cheaper. In fact, Norway is considering making great strides in this sphere. It is said that Norway is considering a ban on sales of vehicles powered by fossil fuels by 2025. It is also aiming to pass a law that would need for new private cars, LCVs, and buses to be zero-emission by the same time. Norway already boasts of electric cars accounting for 24% of the new car market. [16]

It can be easy to marvel at such a forward-thinking Norway. However, its cultural history can be equally marvelous. It is why our first stop was the Viking Ship Museum, Norway's most important cultural heritage. There are three prominent Viking ships on display. Oseberg was equipped with burial gifts, Gokstad was a fast ship suitable for high sea voyages, and Tune was a warship. The museum gives you insights into the Viking culture and the rich sailing heritage of Norway.

Oslo has been the home to Vikings, so the city is filled with historical treasures. But because many of the city's structures were made completely of wood, important city areas have been destroyed by fire several times throughout the years. Christian IV of Denmark determined that the old city should not be rebuilt after the final fire in 1624, which lasted three days. In Akershagen, near Akershus Castle, his troops erected a network of roadways. He insisted that all inhabitants relocate their businesses and workplaces to the newly constructed city of Christiania, which was named after the monarch.

---

[16] https://www.autocar.co.uk/car-news/green-cars/norway-considers-ban-petrol-and-diesel-cars-2025

Viking Museum, Norway

Shipbuilding and trade boosted the city's income following the Great Northern War in the 18th century. Oslo became a commercial port as a result of the booming industry.

Oslo has a wide range of architectural styles. The city has buildings from all major historical construction periods: pre-industrial antiquity to modern-day marvels. Most visitors to the town are likely to consider its architecture very modern. After all, it was only established in the 1800s. When Christiania was designated as the capital of Norway in 1814, there were almost no structures fit for the many new government organizations. A large-scale construction project was started, but due to financial restrictions, it was completed slowly.

With its own international airport, Oslo, with its 23 million population, is well-positioned to become a leading global hub for shipping and logistics. Run by the local council, Oslo has evolved into a major center for finance, industry, technology, and learning. Oslo's reputation as a global hub is backed by strong government initiatives, including developing a free trade zone and excellent infrastructure. Oslo is an expensive place to reside. Yet, it continues to attract those seeking homes for sale and new residents with its dynamic social and economic climate. Oslo is home to several important museums and galleries. The infamous *Scream* and other paintings by Edvard Munch may be found in the Munch Museum, which was donated to the museum post his death.

The extraction and exploitation of Norway's vast oil and gas reserves has been the biggest contributor to the Norwegian economy. It has been the case since they were first discovered in the 1960s. If you consider the fact that this country generates almost 98% of its electricity from renewable energy like hydropower. The knock-on effect is seen thus when most of the oil and gas extracted is exported.

It is estimated that these exports add up to 17% of the national GDP. For further perspective, Norway sells almost $100 billion worth of crude and refined petroleum and petroleum gas. However, Norway cannot keep staying in the status quo. The records show that their gas reserves are slowly reaching the apex from their peak in 1999.

Even as Norway begins to ponder upon these disappearing sources and energy requirements, the areas near the Arctic Circle have gained immense geopolitical significance due to the presence of huge reserves of oil and gas. The challenge of extracting these resources paired with the environmental causes has seen the company shift its focus.

As I mentioned earlier, hydropower charges most of the power grid within this country. In fact, it will be one of the few countries that will not be thrown into chaos and the dark ages when oil finally runs out. The decision taken by Norway to invest public resources into renewable energy seems one prudent decision.

While this does present a rosy picture, Norway still has room for growth. Let us examine the fact that 98% of electricity generated comes from renewable hydropower. If we were to take a pause, a closer perusal will reveal that only 65% of the energy is consumed domestically. Norway is among the frontrunners in renewable energy and there are bound to be a few stumbles. For instance, let's take a look at privately-owned cars. We understand that electric vehicles are on the rise. However, if Norway bled and every citizen was forced to swap out their vehicles with electric vehicles, it would struggle to cope as there would not be enough charging facilities. However, the good news also lie in the fact that Norway could have 100% renewable energy and also produce a surplus by 2030!

Another popular industry in Norway is attached to its geographical location. The long coastline of the country with excellent climate conditions and wide seabeds makes the seafood industry a critical part of this country.

It is estimated that it is the second biggest contributor to Norway's GDP. Norway boasted global sales of over $10 billion in 2016. That figure puts the Scandinavian nation Norway second only to China in seafood exports. If you wish to really appreciate the magnitude when you realize that a country contributes almost 10% of the entire global seafood market with only 0.07% of the global population!

Atlantic salmon is far and away the leading fish exported. The boom in the salmon market is mostly down to the increasing consumption of sushi around Europe. Other popular fish for export include trout, fresh and frozen codfish, and mackerel. In shellfish, prawns and king crabs lead the way.

Lunch for Norwegians is commonly a small open-faced sandwich called matpakke, with each slide separated by several miniature wax paper sheets called mellomleggspapir.

Sailing in Oslo

They take two slices of bread and thinly spread each with butter to make an excellent Matpakke. The liver spread, jam, cheese, or caviar is then added to the butter. Brunost, a slice of traditional dark cheese, is used as an ideal topping for matpakke. Dinner in a conventional home is normally finished up by 5 p.m. and comprises potatoes and meats. This was very surprising to me. You could ask, "Don't Norwegians ever get bored?" But the Norwegians are very active people, always energized to fight the harsh climate. I was surprised to see over 50 Indian restaurants listed in Oslo; we were highly recommended to visit a couple of them. We were quite impressed by how close the food's taste matched the tastes back home. However, to have a traditional Norwegian dinner is another thing altogether.

In the early years, Norwegian food was mostly prepared around fishing and hunting as the supply lasted all year round.[17] Norwegian food comes very close to Finnish food. It has a similar taste, style

---

[17] https://talknorway.no/food-history-the-beginning-norway/

and, as a result, is often confusing to non-Norwegians.

The most popular dish is Mutton and cabbage stew, or "fårikål" in Norwegian. The word Farikal means sheep in cabbage. Farikal is served with potatoes, carrots, cowberry sauce, and flatbread. It uses a variety of spices, most prominently cayenne pepper, to give it a spicy kick. Cowberries are popular in Norweigian cuisine.

Village Life in Norway

We went to a nice Norwegian restaurant and asked the chef for some tips on preparing a great Farikal. She told us the trick lies in adequately covering the meat with flour and layering it with meat, cabbage, and peppercorns. It also depends on how efficiently hot water is poured and the cooking time. Typically, it needs 2-3 hours to make meat and cabbage tender in a tight lid. Temperature control is essential to avoid burning or overcooking the meat or cabbage. We ate at Gamle Raadhus Restaurant, located in the heart of the city. I was apprehensive since it was my first-time sampling reindeer. But after that, I proceeded to polish dollops of my favorite Movenpick ice cream next to a fountain welcoming the lovely seagulls.

Flam & Bergen:

From Oslo, we journeyed to Flam. The Flam voyage was one of the most incredible experiences I have ever had on a trip. In a nutshell, Norway and the journey across the Fjords are unforgettable experiences.

You are likely to imagine a dramatic landscape of snow-covered peaks and glaciers when you think of Norway. But the country is much more varied than that image. I was transported to different worlds on my journey to Flam.

It is a trip that combines a train ride and a cruise with stops in fairy-tale lookalike villages. If there is one journey I could go back and experience again, it will always be Flam. When you stand on the deck of an electric boat, staring out at a dreamlike panorama, with the fresh fjord breeze in your hair, you will feel like you are in a movie.

The Flam Railway is one of the world's most beautiful train journeys. The view from the train as it glides through the tropical jungle is enough to take your breath away. The train passes through small settlements and keeps its distance from the factories and other buildings that line the tracks.

While the train itself is beautiful, it is the journey that matters. Those few hours spent riding through the jungle remind you that life is fragile and that every moment counts. We also took a fjord cruise on Nærøyfjorden, Aurlandsfjorden, and the Nærøydalen valley, which is also a UNESCO World Heritage Site. By creating unique experiences and selling them to the market, Flåm has positioned itself as a premium travel destination.

Fjords and mountains are synonymous with Norway. This experience is tailored to individuals who desire an intense day trip or who want to spend many days exploring fjord Norway. The journey began on schedule in Oslo, and the train passed past some of the most breathtaking sights. A halt at the Kjosfossen waterfall is one of the greatest photo chances on this route.

Natural springs on the journey through the fjords

We stepped off the train to walk to the observation platform for a break, and out of the woods appeared a mysterious woman with long hair and a scarlet outfit, dancing to a Norwegian folk tune. She is the Huldra, a forest spirit from mythology. She lures men into the woods per local culture to seduce them. I was a bit shaken, only for our guide to tell us that this was an act to recreate legend by the local ballet school.

Even in June, the Flam terminal had wonderful stores where one could get some truly warm woolens. We left early in the morning and stayed in Aurland, where we did fjord kayaking. We took a cruise from Flam to Bergen the next day, sailing through the Sognefjord, Norway's longest and deepest fjord.

Bergen is a peaceful town with a lovely downtown area. Because it gets dark around 11 p.m. and there are rays of light as early as 2 a.m., one might roam late into the night. The city is a national hub for higher education, media, tourism, banking, and a worldwide center for aquaculture, shipping, the offshore petroleum sector, and subsea technology. The city is home to some of the world's largest aquaculture enterprises, including Mowi and Lery. Financial institutions are well-represented in the city. The city is home to the banks Sbanken and Sparebanken Vest. Bergen has a large distribution of newspapers, circulating to up to 30k+. The Bergen Philharmonic Orchestra, formed in 1765, and the Bergen Woodwind Quintet perform at Grieg Hall, the city's primary cultural venue. Carte Blanche, Norway's national contemporary dance group, is also based in the town.

Norway is a land of visual wonder, with towering peaks and pristine valleys. The country is home to some of the most stunning natural scenery in the world, and its landscapes are truly a sight to behold. From the snow-capped mountains to the glistening glaciers, Norway is a country that will take your breath away. Norway is a nature lover's paradise. With its vast and varied landscapes, Norway is also a photographer's dream. There is something about Norway that is so unique and breathtaking. The fjords are a big part of what makes this country so visually stunning. They are long, narrow inlets that were formed by glaciers. And they are surrounded by towering cliffs that are just begging to be explored.

The best way to experience the fjords is by boat. And there are plenty of companies that offer tours. You can choose a calm and relaxing ride, or an adrenaline-pumping adventure. Whichever you choose, you are sure to be amazed by the beauty of the fjords. If you are lucky enough to visit Norway, do not miss out on the opportunity to see the fjords.

Haugastol

They are truly a sight unmatched and unrivaled. Norway is a country of incredible natural beauty, with something to offer everyone. With its towering mountains, pristine lakes, and dramatic coastline, there is a huge range of activities on offer, from hiking and skiing in the mountains to kayaking and fishing in the lakes and fjords. The country is also home to some of the most stunning scenery in the world, with the Aurora Borealis lighting up the night sky in winter and the Midnight Sun shining during summer. Whether you are looking for adventure or simply want to relax in beautiful surroundings, Norway is the perfect destination.

9

RUSSIA

*You will not grasp her with your mind
Or cover with a common label,
For Russia is one of a kind –
Believe in her, if you are able…*
— Fyodor Tuchaev

Russia is the largest country in the world and was a former member of the USSR. It is a country of many titles. It is one of the most powerful countries globally with its natural gas reserves, coal reserves, and unmatched military force supported by its nuclear arsenal. However, when one visits Russia, all these things take a back seat. Its scenic beauty and onion-domed architecture will take your breath away. The country certainly has seen many wars and rulers. You will get that sense with every monument and street. They hold great historical significance.

We started our Russian odyssey when our Finnair flight landed in St Petersburg from Helsinki. If you have noticed, I am fascinated by museums and the many untold stories within them. I have been fortunate to visit some of the most iconic museums like the Louvre, and History Museum and I was most looking forward to visiting Hermitage. Spread across six buildings, the Hermitage in St Petersburg is one of the largest museums on this planet. From ancient Egyptian artifacts to paintings by Leonardo da Vinci, the Hermitage has it all. It was founded in 1764 by Catherine the Great and houses over three million works of art, making it one of the largest collections in the world. The museum is spread out over six buildings, including the Winter Palace, and covers an area of over six hectares. It is located in the city center of St Petersburg, Russia on the bank of the Neva River. It has been open to the public since 1852. I remember seeing paintings by some of the most famous artists in the world, including Leonardo da Vinci, Rembrandt, and Picasso. The Madonna Litta by da Vinci, Titian's Danae, Pissarro's Two Sisters (Meeting), and Rembrandt's The Return of the Prodigal Son are among the masterpieces in the collection. The Winter Palace was the former residence of the Russian tsars. A visit to the Hermitage is a step back in time to a world of opulence and luxury.

The Hermitage

While the Hermitage was founded by Catherine the Great, it actually started as her private art collection. It is said that she bought over 200 pieces of artwork in 1764 alone. The museum only opened for public viewing in 1852. There is one more thing that makes this museum unique compared to other museums. It employs about 50 to 70 cats that live in the museum to catch mice. They were first brought to the Winter Palace by Elizabeth I, the daughter of Peter the Great. The museum today is recognized for its emerald green and white colors of the exterior walls. These colors are its modern iteration as it has been painted in different colors throughout history from pale yellow to brick red.

We managed to get ourselves a lovely homestay opposite St Isaac's Cathedral, the largest Orthodox Bascilia. The building is an architectural marvel. It is one of the most iconic and beautiful landmarks in St. Petersburg. The cathedral was designed by Auguste de Montferrand and took 40 years to build, from 1818 to 1858. It is one of the largest cathedrals in the world and can accommodate up to 14,000 people. The exterior of the cathedral is adorned with incredible sculptures and the interior is lavishly decorated with paintings and mosaics. I couldn't hlp but be amazed by the exterior of the cathedral which is adorned with intricate details and impressive statues, while the interior is just as breathtaking with its soaring ceilings and grandiose artwork. No matter where you stand, inside or outside of the cathedral, you can't help but be in awe of its beauty.

I found the facade of the cathedral particularly impressive, with its ornate golden statue of an angel on the top of the central dome. The angel is said to symbolize the highest point that a human being can reach. The facade is also decorated with numerous statues and reliefs of biblical scenes. The interior of the cathedral is no less impressive, with its massive columns and beautifully painted frescoes. The cathedral also houses a valuable collection of icons and other religious artifacts.

Its architecture is a mix of Byzantine and Baroque styles. One of the most impressive features of the cathedral is its roof. The roof is made up of 12 large copper domes that are covered in gold leaf. The domes are arranged in a cross shape and they are surmounted by a tall cross. The roof is one of the most photographed features of the cathedral and it is truly a sight to behold.

When I entered the interior of St. Isaac's Cathedral, my breath had a catch as I was immediately awed by the height of the nave and the grandeur of the iconostasis. The iconostasis is made of marble and is absolutely massive, yet intricately beautiful. One can't help but be impressed by the skill of the artists who created it. The whole interior of the cathedral is breathtaking and leaves one feeling humbled by its beauty. The nave is the central part of the cathedral and is supported by massive columns. The walls are decorated with beautiful paintings and mosaics. The cathedral also has a large organ that is used for musical performances. I was also able to ascend to the top of the cathedral for a stunning view of the city. Another particular highlight during my St Petersburg trip was the visit to the Fabergé Museum to see the world-renowned Fabergé Eggs. The Fabergé Eggs were a series of 50 eggs made by Peter Carl Fabergé from the jewelry firm The House of Fabergé. The Russian imperial Romanov family commissioned these intricate and ornate eggs every Easter.

Peterhof Palace

The summer palace of Peter the Great – the Peterhof Palace was another amazing place. We chose to go there by boat. As the name suggests, this palace served as the summer residence for the first Russian Emperor, Peter the Great. The Palace was a gorgeous and rich place with fantastic art, including Peter the Great's prints, paintings, furniture, and clothing. It also features the sculptures of Adam and Eve.

One place I absolutely loved was Nevsky Prospekt. It is the main street in the city of Saint Petersburg. It is named after the Neva River, which flows through the city. The street runs from the Admiralty to the Alexander Nevsky Monastery. It is the busiest street in the city and is full of shops, restaurants, and cafes. There are also a number of nightclubs and bars.

While there were shops and bars, I was more taken by its grand architecture, high-end shops, and lively nightlife. We had chosen the best time to shop on Nevsky Prospekt – during the day, when the sun was shining and the shops were open. I found all the high-end brands as well as plenty of Russian goods.

For the best shopping deals, I would recommend that you head to Gostiny Dvor, one of the city's largest shopping malls. There you will find all the major Russian and international brands. If you are looking for a more unique shopping experience, check out some of the small boutiques and specialty shops along Nevsky Prospekt. If you're looking for more affordable shopping, check out the second-hand shops on Dumskaya Ulitsa. You can find some great bargains on clothing, books, and other items here.

There is no better way to see St Petersburg than the midnight cruise. The city has dozens of canals that act as arteries to connect with the imposing River Neva. These canals also feature pick-up points for those who wish to take the midnight cruise. The cruise itself begins at around 11:30 pm. It will take you through narrow canals to the River Neva. One of the most amazing sights is when you see the bridge over the river creak open from the middle. The bridge's illuminated ends open fully and strike a dramatic pose against the blue sky.

Bridge opening at midnight

You did not read the last sentence wrongly. The sky is still blue and not dark at midnight. Sunsets in St Petersburg happen well past midnight at around 2 am.

When I took the cruise, the city seemed so different, it felt alive. Even as I sat and took a sip of my coffee and I took in the sights for the next hour-and-half, I could not help but marvel at the city. It was twilight and there was an air of romance. It could also have been the aromas of the delicious five-course meal that I had on board. The cruise will take you past all of the major landmarks, including the Spit of Basil Island, Mikhailovsky Castle, and the glittering Trinity Bridge.

St Petersburg supports Russia as an economic gateway and is Russia's financial and industrial center. It served the country with expertise in oil and gas trade, shipbuilding yards, aerospace industry, technology, including radio, electronics, software, and computers; machine building, heavy machinery, transport, instrument manufacture, metallurgy, and many more. With these capabilities, St. Petersburg accounts for about 15% of the total Russian GDP and about 28% of its exports. St. Petersburg has undergone tremendous expansion as a result of its geographical position. Its population has boomed from 1.5 to 2.5 million people since 1990. This growth has been fueled by high disposable incomes, growing house prices, and high levels of foreign investment.

The port of Petersburg facilitates trade between countries. Additionally, the riverports are a great advantage to St. Petersburg as it is the key link between the Baltic Sea and the rest of Russia via the Volga-Baltic Waterway.

Its strategic location on the Baltic Sea is beneficial to domestic and international investors. It is a global financial center and one of the top-20 cities for international visitors. St. Petersburg is home to many foreign businesses as a prominent Russian city. These businesses include multinationals from the United Kingdom, the United States, Canada, and other countries. Companies like Opel, Hyundai, and Nissan have agreed to develop vehicle manufacturing facilities near Saint Petersburg in collaboration with the Russian government. The automotive and auto-parts industries have been growing steadily in this city during the recent decade.

It is no secret that Russians love beer and vodka. The brewery and distillery industry has also been increasing at a rapid rate. St. Petersburg is known as Russia's Beer Capital and contributes to its economy enormously. In the last decade, the amount of beer produced in the country has doubled.

Saint Petersburg has evolved into a one-of-a-kind repository of European architectural styles from the previous three centuries. The city features some of the most iconic buildings globally, dating as far back as the 1500s. Set against the backdrop of those beautiful old buildings, these UNESCO-listed parts of the city are transformed into a modern plaza for visitors to enjoy. Improbably, St. Petersburg has risen from the rubble of World War II and the Soviet Union to become one of the world's most innovative and beautiful cities.

The culinary history of St. Petersburg, Russia, dates back more than 300 years to the days when Peter the Great founded the city on a dry island in the Gulf of Finland. Since then, St. Petersburg has played a pivotal role in developing Russian cuisine.

With more than 3,000 restaurants and adequate hotels, St. Petersburg is currently the 15th most popular city for culinary visitors. It is also one of the most accessible places with airports and seaports that can handle more than 15 million visitors a year. As a result, St. Petersburg has become a significant player on the international stage of culinary tourism, with guests from all over the world enjoying its vibrant energy and diverse offerings. Traditional cuisines and regional specialties abound in St. Petersburg.

Whether you follow your favorite chef to the kitchen or order takeout from your favorite restaurant, you can be sure to find a variety of dishes to enjoy. St. Petersburg is known as the birthplace of Russian cuisine. The chicken Kyiv, fried chicken breasts filled and wrapped in eggs and breadcrumbs, was one of the meals that became an instant hit in Petersburg and beyond. It was a hit for me too. The chicken had a tangy flavor from the extra butter and herbs. Despite its name, the dish is not named after Kyiv of Ukraine but rather originated from the city of St. Petersburg itself. One of the first restaurants to specialize in Kyivs was established in St. Petersburg in 1972. Shortly thereafter, the dish became more accessible and increasingly popular.

St. Petersburg's restaurant scene mixes seafood with a variety of regional delicacies. The Galley, in particular, was a restaurant that served artisan beers (which my father likes) and substantial fare. The nautical theme in the restaurant's décor was a suitable complement to the city's marine aspect due to its location. However, there is one fun observation I had in St Petersburg. The best KFC chicken burger I ever had was here. I have gone to the seemingly ubiquitous KFC franchises around the world. However, none were as juicy as the one in St Petersburg.

After St Petersburg, we had a one-day stay in the small town of Rosa Kuttur. Ros Kuttur was once an Olympic village. However, the highlight of the trip was Rts Galaktika, a water park. This place revealed the child in my father. We went on countless water rides and remember the fun we shared with friends. It was the exact thing we needed for a break. Exhausted after our rides, we polished multiple chicken Kyiv after. After our brief stop at Rosa Kuttur, we went to Sochi. Sochi is located on the shores of the Black Sea and we stayed on the beachfront. If Rts Galatika was the amusement, Sochi and the Black Sea provide the excitement. It is a fun place great for water sports. I thoroughly enjoyed my time here and the most memorable event was my first experience of paragliding from a boat.

Paragliding in Sochi

The place is virtually open till 4 am or more and if you ever feel hungry, there are eateries on the beach that will with various foods. Sochi also gave me another first. I experienced what it feels like to go to a World Cup match.

The date was 16 June 2018. Portugal played Spain and I realized what a carnival and spectacle the Word Cup were and how a sport is celebrated (often over the top).

After the excitement at Sochi, we flew to Moscow. The World Cup fever was still prevalent as Moscow was dressed like a carnival. As the hotels were full, we could only find accommodations outside the city. However, I feel that it was a blessing in disguise. The city was caught up in the World Cup excitement leaving us with the chance to explore the famous Moscow metro and its maze of underground markets (the underground markets were built to brave the harsh winters) Some of the stations themselves are a work of art; I still remember the mesmerizing beauty of Arbatskaya Station.

Moscow at night

Moscow is the largest metropolis in Europe. Moscow's most appealing qualities are its inventive tradition, rich culture, and magnificent architecture. It is one of Europe's most bustling cities, with a potent mix of history and edginess. St. Basil Cathedral, the Moscow Kremlin, the Bolshoi Theatre, and the Red Square are just a few fascinating and intriguing attractions to visit in Moscow during the summer. The Red Square's ambiance was amiable, and it is undoubtedly Russia's most famous iconic landmark. It separates the Kremlin walls and the Kitay Gorod commercial district in the heart of Moscow. We went there for the FIFA World Cup, and the city had been transformed into a massive carnival, the likes of which I had never seen before. People from all around the globe were partying and soaking in the spirit of the World Cup.

We snuck onto the Ritz Carlton's rooftop, where the view of Red Square and the Kremlin was stunning. I also got a chance to eat my favorite Greek salad at the restaurant. Exploring the Moscow Metro was a once-in-a-lifetime experience, as it provided profound insights into the city's navigation system and map through its underground infrastructure. Trains and Russia are a heady mix. Russia is known for having the longest railway route and its metro network.

Until the 1930s, Moscow used horse carried barrows as a means of transportation. When the Metro made its entrance, it instantly became the focal transport point. It was also a means for the Soviets to demonstrate their technological might. It is not just the effectiveness of the system. Some of the stations are spectacular in their splendor. The subways were also designed so that the public would be submerged in Soviet values and culture. The chandeliers, art, and mosaic compilations make it impossible to believe they are, perhaps, just stations. The metro network is not just aesthetically pleasing, but it also has a substantial economic impact on Moscow.

The city also features many underground markets to combat the cold and long winters. Another interesting facet is the wide roads, which I was told could land planes if required, especially during war. In fact, in 2018, two bomber planes did land on a federal highway, but it was about 1000kms south of Moscow. Nevertheless, a fighter plane landing on the street is a terrifying thought!

Moscow was the capital under the Soviets' rule and was directly impacted by it. The Soviet Union's industry was one of the world's largest, but it was also unreliable and costly to maintain. Joseph Stalin tried to modernize Moscow when he was in power. Stalin's designs for the city featured a network of huge avenues and roads, some of which were over ten lanes wide. But they were built at the price of bringing down a large number of historic structures and districts.

Saint Basil's Cathedral, Moscow

One such monument that was destroyed was the *Sukharev Tower*. Though Stalin's notorious actions cannot be justified, he did turn around the architectural look of Russia. He created a few prominent landmarks. Seven Sisters are seven huge skyscrapers dispersed around the city at equal distances from the Kremlin. They are perhaps, the most renowned monuments of the Stalinist period.

Following the split of the USSR, Russia did not fare well. Moscow did remain Russia's capital. However, the economy deteriorated, and it became imperative that the Russian economy be thoroughly altered. In such circumstances, Moscow started developing a Market-Economy.

Shops, services, architecture, and lifestyles influenced by Western culture began to flourish. Today, Moscow is home to many billionaires and blooming industries. The Mil Moscow Helicopter Plant, the Khrunichev State Research and Production Space Centre, ISS, ICBMs. Sukhoi, Ilyushin, Mikoyan, Tupolev, and Yakovlev are all Moscow. The economic benefit that these businesses provide to Moscow is enormous.

Under the Soviets' rule, the economy of Moscow thrived on industrial manufacturing and agriculture. Soviet-influenced Moscow's economy grew greatly, and hence, Moscow's income is prominently supported by manufacturing industries. The real estate business in Moscow is flourishing, and the rates multiply every year.

Moscow may not be the first thing that pops up when you think of a food destination. But the country is full of delicious, traditional dishes to try. Seafood has been easy to come by as Russia has coast to three major oceans.

However, it doesn't end there. Mushrooms and berries were also consumed in the olden days. Russians are obsessed with bread and porridge. Till the 18th century, no one had even heard about potatoes or tomatoes. The salads were prepared with single vegetables. Soupy dishes appeared a bit later. There was a fish soup, shchi, and later borsch, rassolnik - sour soup, and then came solyanka. It is a traditional local soup stewed with a variety of meats such as bacon, sausage, and ham and vegetables such as carrots, onions, and cabbage. The soup has a delectable sour flavor from a typical lemon sliced garnish and chopped pickles.

Other cuisines famous amongst the locals are Pirozhki, a boat-shaped bun with various fillings to choose from; Ukha, a comforting Russian soup made from different types of fish; Borscht, a beetroot-based soup with slight tanginess to it. Moscow offers the best Russian cuisine: from traditional food places to modern, fine dining destinations.

Pushkin is the best place to visit if you want to experience it and be treated like a Russian aristocracy. The pre-Revolution Russian ambiance is recreated with the aristocratic country décor and the flowery font of the menu. Café Pushkin is one of Moscow's greatest eating places, owing to its exceptional cuisine and service quality.

Russia is a land of contrasts. It is the largest country in the world, spanning nine time zones and two continents. Its history is rich and its culture is unique. From the bustling metropolises of Moscow and St. Petersburg to the rural villages of the countryside, Russia is a country of great beauty and endless possibilities. Russia is a country that has something for everyone. Whether you're interested in the arts, the history, the food, or the nightlife, there's something here for you. The people are friendly and welcoming, and there's always something new to see and do.

10

SWITZERLAND

The mountain sat upon the plain
In his eternal chair,
His observation omnifold,
His inquest everywhere.

The seasons prayed around his knees,
Like children round a sire:
Grandfather of the days is he,
Of dawn the ancestor.'
— The Mountain by Emily Dickenson

I believe every place has its aura, and I have managed to feel it. We've visited many cities, and I know I can distinguish them if I close my eyes and smell the air. When I landed in Switzerland, I was confident that dreams do come true. Switzerland has always been a dream destination for South Asians, let alone Indians.

While savoring the Swiss chocolates, I believed there were chocolate mountains in Switzerland when I was a kid. As a grown-up, I laughed at my innocence, even as the inner child in me hoped to catch a glimpse of one such mountain.

Switzerland is known for its timepieces, cheese, chocolate, fondue, accuracy, engineering, cows, milk, and other products, but its skiing slopes are its main draw. Though visitors rush to Switzerland in the winter, the Alps' slopes convert into some of the most magnificent walks imaginable in the summer.

Since we were in Switzerland, the first thing we did was to see a clock in Bern. We went to see the large and well-known one - Zytglogge, which has been showing the time since 1405. On the other hand, if you want to know what time it is, you should read one of Albert Einstein's writings, which were published in the city. He resided a short distance from the clock. He created an array of four publications that shocked the scientific world in 1905: Photoelectric Effect, Brownian Motion, Mass-Energy Equivalence, and Special Relativity, all of which were described in that one incredible year. The most nerve-wracking travel experience we've ever had was climbing up to the little chamber where these Annus Mirabilis documents were composed. If you want a layman's grasp of these concepts, go to the History Museum, where the floor dedicated to Einstein does a good job. We squeezed in a visit to the city's Munster in between these secular outings, ascending the 350-odd stairs to the summit of Switzerland's highest tower for some dizzying vistas. We're not the "views are quickly gratified" kind. But I was stunned by its majesty. Any lyrical superlatives succumb without a struggle in face of the pure majesty of incomprehensible natural beauty in the Berner Oberland, the pulsating heart of the Swiss Alps. We went down to the lakes, which are at the base of the mountain range, Lake Brienz and Lake Thun, with the touristic Interlaken sandwiched in between. We first crossed Brienz to reach Meiringen on the opposite side, which is home to the 250-meter-high Reichenbach Falls, which has been famous since 1893 as the location selected by Arthur Conan Doyle to assassinate Sherlock Holmes. In the afternoon, we drove across Lake Thun to the town of Thun, which is known for its fairy-tale castle, also called Thun. Built in the 1180s, the fortress passed through several owners until settling securely in the hands of the

Bernese in the late 14th century. To say the least, the views from the castle keep of the lovely town and the Oberland beyond were stunning.

When we stepped onto Lucerne, I realized, that Lucerne is one of the most livable cities I've ever visited after just one day. Despite the large number of visitors who flock to the city on summer days, it is a clean city with well-manicured greens, an emerald green Lucerne Lake glistening right in the heart of the city, and cool summer breezes from the Alps. It is an old city made up of traditional European houses neatly lined up in beautiful colors, and best of all, a pedestrian and bike-friendly city. Bikes paths have been established all over the city, and we observed a lot of cyclists wandering the city in harmony with the light traffic.

Chapel Bridge, Lucerne

Automobiles (even huge trucks) wait whenever pedestrians cross the road, a wonder I've never seen before. I've never felt safer on the road in a strange city before. We did the golden round trip in Lucerne, Switzerland, on Mount Pilatus, one of the Swiss Alps.

We went for a boat trip on Lake Lucerne, where the pure emerald green lake glistened in the sunlight. Traditional homes from the ancient town dotted the valleys and up the hill as we rode, creating a pleasant and calm landscape in the gorgeous lake area.

Titlis, Engelberg

We then arrived at Alpnachstad, at the foot of Mount Pilatus, after a 40-minute boat journey, and looked up to see fluffy white clouds climbing up the Pilatus Kulm, the mountain's snow-covered peak. We took a steep 45-degree train trip up to Pilatus Kulm, and the train was cleverly engineered with a ladder-like incline to keep people from feeling dizzy. The train rumbled through high cliffs, vast green valleys that dropped like a sheet of green carpet, clouds, and into the Pilatus Kulm, which was surrounded by white sheets of seemingly unmelted glass. I took long breaths breathing in the air of the Swiss alps, which were fresh, cool, and pristine. We took a trek to the top of the Pilatus, where beautiful valleys dipped into the sky and the Lucerne Lake could be seen in the distance. As we struggled up the route, we felt wonderful and carefree. One of the nicest parts about eating out is that we can converse while the meal is being made. The lunch consisted of classic Swiss fare, such as meatballs with mashed potatoes. They were richly prepared with a cheese-like sauce, blueberries for the meatballs, and melt-in-your-mouth mashed potatoes).

Titlis

We toured the countryside of Lucerne, Engelberg, and neighboring counties, admiring the lovely small houses that dotted the landscape.

After passing through many valleys and breathtaking mountain ridges, I wondered what it's like to live in such a lovely area with pure air, and clean water from the Alps. There is no traffic and there is unfathomable greenness everywhere you turn. We went to the glacier park on the Titlis flyer, which was a cable with our feet suspended in midair.

Gliding across glaciers and snow was a beautiful experience, with a kingdom of white all around us, with thick inches of snow and unfathomable mountain ranges below.

My journey to the dreamland is further intensified now when I am at home replaying these images, brushing my memories, and re-living those days. Switzerland was created in 1291 by an alliance of cantons against the Habsburg dynasty—the Confoederatio Helvetica (or Swiss Confederation), from which the acronym CH for Switzerland derives—but the current nation was formed only in 1848 when a new constitution was ratified. Before 1848, internal conflict was common, but Switzerland has enjoyed relative domestic tranquillity since the mid-nineteenth century. Its organization has remained essentially the same: a union of more than 3,000 communes, or municipalities, spread across 26 cantons, six traditionally referred to as demicantons (half cantons) but functioning as full cantons.

Ordinary individuals can engage in politics at all levels and routinely express their views through referendums and initiatives, which allow Swiss residents to directly influence countless policy choices at the national and sub-national levels. There are two obvious consequences of this widespread involvement: Swiss taxes are low by European standards.

It is because voters may evaluate and approve a wide variety of expenditures, and political decision making is delayed since competing individual claims and viewpoints must be allowed to be aired at every stage. Because of this high degree of citizen engagement, the famed 20th-century Swiss dramatist and ironist Friedrich Dürrenmatt described Switzerland as a jail where every Swiss citizen was both a prisoner and a guard.

Nonetheless, the Swiss combination of federalism and direct democracy is unique globally, and it is seen as critical to the country's political and economic success. And, because of its long legacy of financial services and high-quality, specialized manufacturers of things such as precise clocks, optics, chemicals, and medicines, as well as special delicacies such as Emmentaler cheese and milk chocolate, Switzerland is undoubtedly a great economic force. Switzerland is often ranked as having one of the greatest living standards in the world.

Over the last three centuries, Swiss watchmakers have solidified their position as the world's foremost horologists. Rolex, for example, has built a reputation for outstanding workmanship, ensuring that their watches are the epitome of beauty and sophistication. However, a visit to this charming nation may surprise you to realize that there are nearly 100 manufacturers fighting alongside the big brands. Many of them are still headquartered in the small, attractive Alpine towns of La Chaux-de-Fonds and Le Locle, which were both designated as World Cultural Legacy sites in 2009 for their famous horological heritage. Half of the world's watches were formerly made in this city. Visitors may still explore the workshops and factories, as well as learn the fundamentals of watchmaking by disassembling and reassembling a simple mechanism. If you're not sure how to differentiate a Breguet from a Breitling, here's a quick rundown of some of the country's most well-known brands.

Vulcaine was formed in 1858 and has just 13 employees despite its long and prosperous history. The Jura-based firm is located in Le Locle. Every US president since Dwight Eisenhower in the 1950s has worn one of the company's iconic Cricket watches, which are simply known as "The Presidents' Watch."

With an inspired building design and as a center for innovation, Switzerland now boasts a gorgeous new watch museum. The museum belongs to the Swiss firm Audemars Piguet and is located in the famed Vallee de Joux, which is known for being a center of watchmakers.

The Musee Atelier Audemars Piguet is a spiral-shaped structure in the Jura Mountains of Switzerland. The world-famous Audemars Piguet watch firm began in 1875 when Juls Louis Audemars and Edward Auguste Piguet established their business here. In fact, the museum is just next door to the watchmaker's offices.

You can learn about the history of this Swiss watchmaker at the museum, which also has some of its most famous clocks on exhibit.

The Bjarke Ingels Group developed the fascinating structure, which has a glass structure that connects it to the company's present campus next door. It meshes perfectly with its surroundings because of its grass roof, which also allows plenty of light inside the structure. One of the museum's most appealing features is the opportunity to enter the workrooms where the watches are created and experience the process firsthand.

The Jaeger-LeCoultre Hybris Mechanica à Grande Sonnerie's seven-figure price is due to the watch's incredible engineering. It has 1,300 moving parts that help power perpetual calendars that never need to be adjusted (even in leap years), as well as brilliantly crafted tourbillons – ingenious devices invented two centuries ago to counteract the effects of gravity on a mechanical movement regardless of the angle at which the watch is worn.

Patek Philippe, a Geneva-based family business founded in 1839, is known for its creative designs and fine craftsmanship. The business was the first to develop perpetual calendars for wristwatches. It's also exclusive: most of the 200 models in regular production are limited to just ten pieces. Frédérique Constant, another Geneva-based luxury brand, has created the Horological Smartwatch, which combines old-world craftsmanship with cutting-edge technology.

The handcrafted design connects to a smartphone through Bluetooth and can track and quantify everyday activities including distance traveled, calories burnt, and even sleep monitoring. [18]

---

[18] https://www.telegraph.co.uk/travel/untapped-destinations/where-to-buy-a-watch-in-switzerland/

While discussing the watch industry of Switzerland, how can I forget to mention Geneva and my wonderful experience there? Geneva is Switzerland's second-biggest city and is widely regarded as the world's watch capital, so it's only natural that one of its monuments is a clock constructed of flowers. The Flower Clock, also known as l'Horloge Fleurie, is located in the heart of Geneva, on the outskirts of the English Garden, or Jardin Anglais, on the southern side of Lake Geneva. For over 50 years, the clock has been keeping time and entertaining tourists. Inside the clock, there are a total of 6500 plants, and full-time gardeners transplant the blooms each season, ensuring that the colors change throughout the year. The Flower Clock is a five-meter-diameter clock with a circumference of 15.7 meters and is one of Geneva's most photographed attractions. Its second hand, measuring 2.5 meters (8.2 feet), holds the record for being the world's longest. The clock's initial design was much smaller and consisted of only one circle, but it was redesigned in 2002 and currently consists of eight concentric flowery circles.

Geneva features around 50 public clocks and 200 watch retailers since it is the world's leader in watchmaking and clocks. The mechanical clock of the Hôtel Cornavin is one of those fascinating clocks. This clock is the world's highest and attracts a large number of tourists. If you've ever visited Geneva, you've probably seen the Jet d'Eau Fountain, the city's most famous feature. The Jet d'Eau, one of the world's largest fountains and Europe's largest, can even be seen from 30,000 feet in the air. The Jet d'Eau Fountain is the most famous landmark in Geneva, Switzerland. The Rhone River drains into the Jet d'Eau, which is located on Lake Geneva. Its spray reaches a height of 459 feet and has a flow rate of 132 gallons per second. Water leaves the nozzle at 124 mph and is powered by two 500 kW pumps at 2400 volts. The fountain runs all year except when there are exceptionally high gusts or when the temperature is below 2 degrees Celsius (35.6 degrees Fahrenheit). The fountain, which was originally erected in 1886 at a position downstream, was a safety valve for a hydraulic system and stood at a considerably lesser height of fewer than 100 feet. The fountain was transferred to its current site five years later, at which point the height of the fountain had expanded to about 300 feet.

Jet d'Eau

Since significant people began to visit this location, its worth as a tourist attraction has been recognized. The current fountain, which was built in 1951, is one of Geneva's most well-known sights. When I first saw the Jet d'Eau Fountain in Geneva, I was blown away, and as I traveled around the massive lake, I was astounded that I could still see it from afar. Closer inspection revealed tourists who had ventured out onto a pier to get a closer look at the fountain than those who had only seen it from the lakeside. If you opt to view the fountain from this vantage point, be prepared to get wet depending on the changing winds!

Geneva's Old Town is the epicenter of all things historical, so include time in your itinerary to enjoy some eating and shopping in the picturesque city center. Visit Place Bourg-de-Four for museums, boutiques, restaurants, and the greatest Swiss chocolate you've ever tasted! After seeing Old Town from the ground level, ascend to the pinnacle of the iconic Saint-Pierre Cathedral for a great perspective of the city.

Aside from the excellent weather and the lovely and clean ancient town, Geneva Lake is a must-see. Lake Geneva is a deep lake shared by Switzerland and France on the north side of the Alps. It is one of the biggest lakes in Western Europe and the largest on the Rhône's route. Geneva Lake is relatively long, with a great marina harbor and a spectacular fountain visible from many parts of Geneva. Transportation Geneva tickets are accepted by the yellow boats that can whisk you from one store to another in record time. Walking down the bright promenade near the beach is also an incredible experience. The lake is surrounded by mountains and is breathtakingly beautiful. Swimming is permitted on the sandy shores of Geneva Lake.

Because of the various international organizations that have their headquarters in Geneva, it is known as the "city of peace." The United Nations and the International Red Cross, both established in the city, are the most well-known examples. The International Red Cross and Red Crescent Movement were founded in 1863 by a Geneva citizen named Henry Dunant, who formed the ICRC with three other citizens.

The ICRC is the origin of the International Red Cross and Red Crescent movement, which today includes the ICRC, the National Societies, and their International Federation. A few medieval structures and squares may be seen in the old town. Saint Peter's Cathedral, which was built between 1150 and 1230, comprises Romanesque and Gothic aspects as well as a neoclassical grand portico. It is next to the Maccabees Chapel, Geneva's earliest example of flamboyant Gothicism. Aside from its historical significance, the Cathedral has held a special spiritual significance since 1536, when it became a significant Reformation center under John Calvin. It is presently Geneva's most popular tourist attraction. Climbing the North and South towers, which provide a spectacular perspective of the city, is particularly intriguing.

We arrived at the Bourg-de-Four, which is located in the center of Geneva's Old Town, just a few steps from St Peter's Cathedral. Even in the past, highways going to Geneva had to pass via Bourg-de-Four, whose market has been significant since the 9th century. House heights were gradually increased to accommodate Protestant refugees from around Europe.

Don't forget to pay a visit to this charming plaza. Stop in for a cup of coffee or a drink and soak in the atmosphere that the people of Geneva adore. St. Peter's Basilica, which was built between 1160 and 1232, is a cornerstone of religion for the people of Geneva.

The cathedral has been restored multiple times, including a variety of architectural styles: the outstanding façade features white columns in the Greek Corinthian style, similar to those seen in Greek shrines. The Romanesque main architecture of the church includes Gothic spires and arches, making it rather unusual.

A historic chamber may be seen at Geneva's Town Hall. Under the moniker "Alabama", Geneva's international mission rose to prominence in the nineteenth century. It hosted the arbitration tribunal to conclude the war between the United States of America and the United Kingdom in 1872. It was also where the first Geneva Convention – the foundation act of the International Committee of the Red Cross – was signed in 1864.

Watches and knives are the most popular products in Switzerland. Shops sell these things around the country. Aside from watches and knives, Swiss skincare and handicrafts are also worthwhile purchases. Chocolate and sweets are excellent gifts for family and friends. Every year, Switzerland ranks first for chocolate consumption per capita. Every Swiss person consumes 12 kilograms of chocolate each year on average. High-quality ingredients are used to make high-quality chocolate in Switzerland. Whether it's chocolate created in the Lindt and Frey factories or fine handcrafted chocolate produced by small local companies, travelers love Swiss chocolate. Swiss chocolate is a fantastic souvenir and gift option. Any shop in Switzerland will have wonderful chocolate, chocolate desserts, or chocolate ice cream.

Sprüngli, a Zürich-based firm, comes highly recommended. Sprüngli retail stores can be located across Switzerland, including train stations and airports. It is uncanny how my inner child got her dream fulfilled yet again. Though it was not a chocolate mountain, I tasted the chocolate pebble from the hills of my dream. It is also a well-known fact that the Swiss Army knife has become a symbol of Switzerland. Its small size, mobility, and versatility make it ideal for giving as a gift to family and friends. Victorinox and Wenger are two of the most well-known brands. Swiss Army knives have a versatile design that allows them to be used for various tasks. The SwissChamp knife, which has 33 functions, is the most well-known. Swiss Army knives are sold in practically all Swiss cities and tourist locations, and the pricing is usually the same.

Apart from the fantastic views, historical places, and flourishing Economy, Switzerland has one more thing to boast about: its cuisine. There are several eateries in the city we visited during our stay. We had Raclette (cheese). Melted cheese accompanied by "Gschwellti" (jacket potatoes), cocktail gherkins, onions, and pickled fruit. Älplermagronen is a gratin made of potatoes, macaroni, cheese, cream, and onions.

Because Geneva is a city, there is a wide variety of authentic ethnic cuisine. Everyone's tastes vary, but you can't go wrong with these suggestions! Grab a pint of Peruvian beer, don't worry; I chose my americano and had an amazing chicken supper at Miski, Lebanese food at Arabesque (one of the finest Lebanese restaurants I've ever tasted!), refined Japanese cooking at Umami by Michael Roth, or classic Latin cuisine at Alma Restaurant.

You receive a true raclette, with the cheese melted over an open flame in the kitchen. In the center of the old town, it is a site that still seems historical. In the summer, the sun sets about 9-10 p.m., so an evening walk in the fresh air, surrounded by sparrows and falcons, may be quite revitalizing. We entered Hotel D'Angletere, which offered an enthralling view of Lake Geneva and Mont Blanc and served an amazing selection of teas with pastry. We enjoyed a delicious Moelleux Au Chocolat with our coffee.

Our next destination was Chamonix. Chamonix is located in the northwest corner of the Alps, about 15 kilometers from the Italian and Swiss borders. Chamonix and its surrounding valley are encircled by the Mont Blanc range in the south and the Aiguilles Rouges, or red peaks, in the north.

Chamonix

The 17-kilometer-long glacier-carved valley extends from the Col des Montets in the north to the Taconnaz river in the south. The town's center is 1035 meters above sea level, whereas the highest community in the valley's upper reaches is Le Tour, at 1462 meters. The Arve River flows through Chamonix before joining the Rhone in Geneva. Chamonix, one of the most well-known ski destinations in the French Alps, experiences exceptionally harsh winters due to its high altitude, resulting in plenty of snowfall. From November through April, the ski season is in full swing. February and March are the snowiest months. Summers in this part of the world are hot, but they may also be damp. Chamonix's climate is frequently humid.

The region has its unique microclimate, with a wide range of weather on any given day. Thunderstorms may appear out of nowhere.

The valley's glaciers occupy an area of 125 square kilometers. Large woods divide the glaciers, surmounted by granite spires carved into obelisks and strewn with ice and snow. Chamonix has a long history of hotels, with the town's first inn opening in 1770. The first luxury hotel was built in 1816, and the sector grew throughout the 1800s. In the early 1900s, three palaces were constructed. Today, travelers may choose from a variety of lodging options in Chamonix.

Chamonix's rise was accelerated by the arrival of rail and road links. The railway line between St. Gervais Le Fayet and Chamonix was inaugurated in 1901. This railway substantially facilitated access and paved the path for winter sports tourism. In 1924, Chamonix hosted the inaugural Winter Olympic Games, prompting the development of several lifts. My ski experience in Chamonix was unforgettable. All the snow and I felt what ants feel on a heap of sugar. I wish I could go back to Chamonix and be amidst snow and fondue! Ah! Have I not told you about my fondue experience yet? I call it the manna of Switzerland. The fondue, a robust pot full of melted cheese in which you dip bits of crusty bread, is perhaps the most well-known Alpine delicacy.

A popular dish in Chamonix mountain restaurants, the recipe varies depending on the chef's personal preferences. Classic cheese fondue is made using a variety of local cheeses (typically reblochon, gruyère, comté, Beaufort, or Emmental), a little garlic and pepper, a splash of alcohol (kirsch, white wine, or a local liqueur), and a pinch of flour to thicken it. Then you may choose from a variety of flavors, like almonds, mushrooms, tomatoes, chilies, and others.

A meat fondue (fondue bourguignonne) is a pot of heated oil. You dip raw seasoned meat chunks until they are cooked to your preference, then serve with various sauces and salad or pickled gherkins. Dessert fondues, which consist of melted chocolate into which you dip fruit, marshmallows, and other goodies, are becoming increasingly popular.

Cheese Fondue

I must say my heart was full; both as a traveler and student of commerce, I have learned a lot from Switzerland. The Swiss bank is the epitome of an instance showing the flourishing economy. The snow-capped mountains, the colorful flowers, and cheese chocolate; I wonder why people seek heaven outside when it is in our world. Switzerland is the land of delicacy and luster. And my readers, you'll be surprised to know I visit this place almost every day. You are probably laughing now, here is the secret; note it down, just close your eyes, and re-live the unforgettable memories just like the way I am returning back to Switzerland through my 'mind palace.'

11

TURKEY

Give Me a Turkish Army. I will Conquer the world.
— Napoléon Bonaparte

There are many fascinating stories about Turkey. One of the more interesting ones involves Santa Claus. Santa Claus' mythology can be traced back hundreds of years to the monk, St. Nicholas. St. Nicholas is said to have been born around 280 A.D. at Patara, near Myra in modern-day Turkey. However, it is merely one of many stories attached to the gift-giving Claus. Many other traditions involve St. Nicholas, most of which involve the procurement of gifts for children on Christmas.

I am not sure how many of these fascinating tales are true, but when I stepped into Turkey, I was fascinated by the whole place. Oh! What wonderful sights, what rich history! The history of Turkey encompasses the records of both Anatolia (the Asian half of Turkey) and Eastern Thrace (the European part of Turkey). In the second century BCE, the Roman Empire took control of these two formerly separate political territories, which later became the basis of the Roman-Byzantine Empire.

A distinction should also be made between the history of the Turkic peoples and the history of the lands that currently comprise the Republic of Turkey during periods preceding the Ottoman Empire. Before the 14th century, the bulk of the population in Anatolia lived in communities independent of the Ottoman Empire. After 1453, the population was gradually drawn into the Empire, and by the 19th century, more than half of the population was living in settlements directly administered by the government. The outlying regions, especially around the Mediterranean, were heavily influenced by foreign powers, especially France and Italy. Following World War I, the two countries clashed twice over control of Nicosia, the capital of Cyprus. The second clash, in 1922, resulted in ethnic conflict and over one million deaths. The peace agreement, which was signed in June 1923, is still in force today, and as a result, Turkey was founded.

I was mesmerized by Turkey the moment I stepped on it. Well, as an avid traveler every little thing fascinates me, but if you see these little things when weaved together, a gorgeous blanket of memories is formed. Now when I am at home it is this blanket that is keeping me warm. I was taken aback by looking at the roads, mosques, lanes, bazaars, the ethnic people, and their cultures.

Pamukkale, Turkey

Did you know one of the finest recent James Bond flicks was largely shot in Turkey? The plot begins with Bond investigating an attack on MI6 in Istanbul, Turkey's capital city. However, at the start of the film, Bond is sunbathing on Calis Beach in Istanbul's Fethiye neighborhood. He gets summoned back to duty shortly after the incident.

James Bond films have always taken spectators to the most exotic destinations on the planet. Istanbul was put on the map with Skyfall, and tourism to the beautiful city is on the upswing.

When I visited these same areas although armed with a camera and not an MI6-issued gun, I felt the thrill. Turkey is located at the crossroads of Europe and Asia and has been inhabited by different civilizations since the Paleolithic epoch, making it one of the greatest destinations to visit for history fans and explorers alike who enjoy roaming about historical sites. Aside from that, the people are really kind, the cuisine is unbelievably excellent, and the cost of travel is quite low. There is no better location to become acquainted with the Middle Eastern culture than Turkey. Even in big cities like Istanbul, Turkey is typically secure for travelers. People are really nice, especially as you travel east.

However, when visiting large touristy destinations such as Istanbul, it is always a good idea to be cautious and conscious of your possessions and surroundings. Petty crimes like bag snatching and pickpocketing still occur in large cities, particularly in busy areas, so keep your possessions close to you when out and about in Istanbul.

There are ancient mosques all around the nation, including some of the most famous imperial mosques of the Ottoman Empire in Istanbul. Some of the better Seljuk era surviving specimens may be found in more out-of-the-way areas and are well worth hunting out. Istanbul is Turkey's biggest city and main seaport. It served as the capital for both the Byzantine and Ottoman empires. The city is on the Bosphorus, where the Bosporus strait meets the Black Sea. It has a population of more than 7 million, making it one of the largest cities in the world.

Like all great cities, Istanbul also has a great cultural legacy. Institutions including museums, art galleries, auction houses, and private residences line the streets of Istanbul. It also has a great cuisine culture and iconic spots like Hagia Sophia, Topkapi Palace, Blue Mosque, Basilica Cistern, Spice Market, and Grand Bazaar. Fittingly, Istanbul was named a U.N. World City in 2005.

Istanbul's historic walled city sits on a triangular peninsula between Europe and Asia. It is not just geographically that Istanbul stands at this crucible. Throughout history, Istanbul has stood amid clashing waves of religion, culture, and imperial power for over 2,500 years. Sometimes it stood as a bridge, sometimes as a barrier. It was one of the world's most sought-after cities throughout history. It has also been one of the world's largest and most important learning centers. It has universities, museums, art galleries, and historic buildings that date back to the 15th century. Istanbul's mosques are home to some of the city's most well-known architecture. It would be impossible to visit Istanbul without viewing at least a handful of them. It's worth mentioning that attending a mosque necessitates adhering to a dress code that mandates women to cover their heads, remove their shoes, and cover their knees or shoulders, though some mosques are more rigorous than others.

Byzantium may have derived its name from Byzas, the commander of the Greeks from Megara. According to folklore, he seized the peninsula from pastoral Thracian tribes and constructed the town in 657 BCE. The city was razed to the ground by the Roman emperor Septimius Severus for opposing him in a civil war in 196 CE. He then rebuilt it and named it Augusta Antonina in honor of his mother. The city remained a part of the Roman Empire until the 13th century, when the Mongols sacked it.

Constantine I picked Byzantium as the new capital of the Roman Empire, dubbing it New Rome, in 324. Following Theodosius I's death in 395 and the definitive split of the Roman Empire between his two sons, the city known as Constantinople became the capital of the Eastern Roman Empire, the last emperor to rule over a united Roman Empire, Constantin made it even stronger. He built a new city, which he named after himself, Constantinople. Today we know it as Istanbul.

Constantinople became the capital of the Eastern Roman (Byzantine) Empire from 705 to 929. It was besieged by the Bulgarians under Khan Asparius in 708 and again by the Arabs under Caliph al-Qa'id in 843. The latter event famously staved off the city's sack for more than a century. However, the Venetians eventually took control of Constantinople.

We opted to spend our first day in Istanbul covering the top advice from the guidebooks, which are mostly based around the Sultanahmet neighborhood of the city, which is home to the Blue Mosque, Topkapi Palace, and Hagia Sophia. The Blue Mosque is still a functional mosque.

We waited in line for a few minutes before removing our shoes at the door and entering. The iconic dome, the mosque's major architectural centerpiece, was completely obscured by scaffolding, which was a genuine pity. The tiles and paintings we could see were magnificent, but we decided to return when it was done to have a closer look.

Sultan Ahmed I commissioned the architect Mehmet Aa to construct the Blue Mosque between 1609 and 1616. It was built to match the massive Hagia Sophia Mosque across Sultanahmet Square as an imperial display of might. It is supported by four "elephant foot" pillars and the central dome (23.5m in diameter and 43m high) is bordered by four semi-domes, giving it a virtual appearance of a square. The inside of the Blue Mosque is decorated with almost 20,000 handmade ceramic Iznik tiles in a variety of tulips, rose, carnation, and lily motifs, and is brightly lighted by 260 windows.

Aside from its immense size and magnificent beauty, one of the most distinguishing features of this Istanbul mosque is its six minarets, as opposed to the two or four seen in most of the city's mosques.

Legend has it that the Blue Mosque was built due to a misunderstanding — when the Sultan ordered altn minaret (gold minarets), the architect misheard alti minaret (six minarets) – an easy error to make! This sparked debate since the Prophet's mosque in Mecca was the only other mosque with six minarets at the time - an issue the sultan solved by ordering a seventh to be built in Mecca.

The Orthodox Church Hagia Sophia used to be located across the plaza from the Blue Mosque. It was turned into a mosque in 1453, and subsequently into a museum. Where there were originally Christian paintings, the conversion appears to be restricted to a few enormous canvases with Arabic inscriptions. The mosaics of Mary and Jesus are still on the wall in large numbers. The Muslim call to prayer has been resonating from Hagia Sophia's minarets since its conversion to a mosque.

The Hagia Sophia, located in the Sultanahmet area, is Istanbul's most renowned mosque. It was erected in the 6th century and is considered a classic Byzantine design. Due to the site's tremendous popularity, it is suggested that you visit when it first opens when there will be less foot traffic and you will be able to get a true feel of the vastness and size of the structure. When Sultan Mehmed II, often known as Fatih or the "Conqueror," conquered Constantinople, he went immediately to Hagia Sophia, declaring it a mosque and ordering it to be safeguarded in perpetuity. Mustafa Kemal Atatürk, the secularist Turkish leader, proclaimed it a museum in 1934 and continues to be today where visitors of any creed and costume are welcome.

In Hagia Sophia, there is a mosaic portraying the Virgin Mary and the newborn Jesus. He did not order the internal mosaic of Mary and Christ, which dates from the ninth century, to be destroyed or covered. Instead, according to Ottoman historians, he stood in amazement, believing that the Christ child's eyes followed him as he wandered around the edifice.

The paintings of Mary and Jesus remained uncovered in the mosque of Hagia Sophia until 1739, despite the fact that human pictures are nearly never encountered in mosque design. The mosaic was plastered over at the time. When the building was converted into a museum in 1934, the plaster was removed.

The centuries-long exhibition might have been a thank-you to the Prophet Muhammad, who is supposed to have saved an image of the Virgin and Christ when destroying pagan monuments at the Kaaba, Islam's holiest site in Mecca, Saudi Arabia.

Medusa in Turkey

Another breathtaking experience was the visit to the Topkapi Palace. The Topkapi Palace in Istanbul houses one of the world's most precious Chinese and Japanese porcelain collections. The palace was erected in the 1460s and served as the imperial family's residence until the mid-nineteenth century. Its outstanding porcelain collection, which goes back to the 13th century and contains over 1,000 pieces of blue and white celadon and above 3,000 pieces of Yuan, Ming, and Vietnamese pottery, including some of the best blue and white specimens from the Ming Dynasty, is now housed at a museum. Much of the collection would have been gifted as presents from visiting dignitaries each time the Ottoman Empire's crown was passed to a new Sultan. Because the overland silk routes were inappropriate for transporting these delicate artifacts, the bulk of this collection would have been transported through the marine silk routes, which passed through the Persian Gulf and the Red Sea.

The Topkapi Museum is presently Istanbul's most visited

museum, with almost three million visitors each year. As a result, lines can be rather long, especially to visit the Imperial Treasury and the Room of the Prophet's Relics. When visiting Topkapi Palace, be sure to see the spoon maker's diamond, which is on display in the treasure department and is the world's fifth-largest diamond at 86 carats. It is supposed to have gotten its name from a fisherman who mistakenly assumed it was glass and traded it for three spoons at a jewelry market. The Harem part of the palace, which was previously the private abode of Ottoman Sultans and their family, has some of the best handcrafted Iznik tiles in Istanbul.

The palace constructions comprise of four transitional courtyards and the surrounding architectural structures while entering the sultanate gate. The first courtyard, known as Alay Square, Hagia Eirene Church, Royal Mint, bakery, hospital, wood warehouse, and wicker manufacturers' residence are among the palace structures surrounded by gardens and squares.

Divan Square, also known as Justice Square, is the palace's second courtyard and is renowned for being the site of state administration. The official meeting spot of the Divan council was Divan-Hümayun (Kubbealt), which was the site of many festivities throughout history, and the treasury was just next to it. The Courtyard also houses the Ward of the "Zülüflü" Guards (The Tressed Halberdiers) and the Royal Stables, which are located behind the Divan construction, the entrance to the Harem close to Kubbealt.

Enderun Courtyard is also the name of the palace's third courtyard. The Sultan's Audience Hall, Enderun Treasure, the Privy Room, and structures like the Palace School built during Sultan Murat III's reign are all located in this region. The Sultan's pavilions and hanging gardens may be found in the fourth courtyard, which is also the last courtyard. The Baghdad and Revan Pavilions, as well as the Iftaree Gazebo, are the most notable and aesthetically sophisticated examples of Ottoman classical mansion architecture in this region. The Mecidiye Pavilion and the Wardrobe Chamber are the palace's final structures, located in the lowest portion of the fourth courtyard.

We walked to the Grand Bazaar after seeing the two main religious monuments and taking a short look at the Topkapi Palace grounds. Turkish delights, coffee, teas, spices, lanterns, textiles, jewelry, and even gadgets may be found here. Prepare yourself for how congested this spot may get, especially if you intend on buying mementos for your stay; it's more or less anticipated that you'll haggle with sellers for a better deal on the item you want to buy. We went in quest of a 'Turkish carpet' for a vast wall in our home.

Turkey is a safe nation to visit, and the further you walk off the main route, the nicer the natives get. Istanbul hosts several museums, including the Museum of Underwater Archaeology, where visitors can learn about the archaeology of the city's renowned water channels. Another prominent museum, the Museum of the Civilization of Byzantium, highlights the cultures of the ancient city. This museum is located in Old Istanbul, a World Heritage Site. Also nearby is the Aya Sofia Archaeological Site, which has been listed as a UNESCO World Heritage Site since 1983.

A border between two continents

The waters that wash the peninsula have long been referred to as the three seas: the Golden Horn, the Bosporus, and the Sea of

Marmara. The Bosphorus strait, a 31-kilometer-long canal that connects the Black Sea to the Sea of Marmara and serves as a natural border between the two continents, separates Istanbul's European and Asian halves. The Bosphorus Bridge and the Fatih Sultan Mehmet Bridge, also known as Bosphorus Bridge II, link the two sides of the Bosphorus, however many tourists choose to visit Istanbul's European side due to its historical significance.

I was fortunate enough to go on a cruise on the Bosphorus. It is the meeting point of Europe and Asia and the center of several civilizations. The Bosphorus strait unites Istanbul, linking its European and Asian halves with blue chameleon strokes. And while the famous body of water has appeared in an uncountable number of films, songs, and Instagram accounts, the Bosphorus' economic and geopolitical importance will always outweigh its cultural influence.

Travelers can also visit the Mingachevir Palace, the residence of the Ottoman Sultans from 1481 to 1516. This palace, which overlooks the Golden Horn, was designated a UNESCO World Heritage Site in 1983. After touring the city, travelers can retreat to their hotel for a night or choose to continue their travel. The Palace also offers short-term rental capacities.

While I was relishing the oriental history and culture of the place through my eyes, and as I walked through these palaces and mosques, all I could visualize was the past reverberating in the present. The alleys the lanes, and the people; how much they enhance the experience of me as a traveler. It is true I also wanted to know about their commerce. The curiosity of a business student kept on asking me about their economy. I realized that the country's position as a major oil and gas transit point goes back decades. Despite some fluctuations, it has remained a significant source of energy for Europe and other markets.

Turkey's strategic location in the Mediterranean makes it a vital entry point for oil and gas supplies to Europe. They flow through Turkey by pipeline via the Ceyhan oil terminal on Turkey's Mediterranean coast. The country is also a major consumer of oil and gas, with industry figures showing that the average Turkish household uses 2800 kcal per day and quite a large amount of oil. It is important to note that the Bosphorus waterway has played an important role in global trade for millennia. It connects the Black Sea to the Sea of Marmara and, eventually, to the Mediterranean via the Dardanelles strait. Around 48,000 boats traverse the waterways, making this location one of the world's busiest nautical gateways. Tourism accounts for around 13% of Turkey's total economy. According to the World Trade Organization, the country was the sixth most popular tourist desStination; the favorable exchange rate was cited as a crucial factor in attracting visitors.

Like all great cities, Istanbul also has a great cultural legacy. Institutions including museums, art galleries, auction houses, and private residences line the streets of Istanbul. Istanbul, Turkey's largest metropolis and the world's fifth-most populous city, is considered European, despite its location on two continents. Istanbul is divided into two halves, one in Europe and the other in Asia.

The smells of Turkish delicacies energized the foodie in me. A stroll around Grand Bazaar and a cup of Turkish coffee are must-dos. The beguiling aromas that greet you at Istanbul's dining establishments are not deceiving. Meze, a Turkish starter, is divine. It consists of cured and seasoned pork, marinated fish, filled mussels, and fried feta cheese. Mezes are served in various forms, including Fava, a mashed bean appetizer, and Muhammara, a puree prepared from pepper paste, walnut, lemon, and pomegranate juice.

I also ate at several restaurants with my guide. They all offered meze, Turkish coffee, and pastries. One of my favorite restaurants was called Heirloom Café. It was a cool and calm restaurant located on the first floor of a shopping center. We sat down at tablecloth-covered tables set in a greenhouse-like room. I ordered the local specialty, crepes filled with spiced butter and cheese. They were delicious and a perfect snack or meal: the Kofte (meat patties) was something I couldn't get enough of. Kelle Paca, a delectable soup comprised of soft lamb's legs and head topped with butter and garlic-lemon sauce, was the perfect symphony for my newly awakened appetite. While in Istanbul, I was captivated by the Güler Ocakbaş & Restaurant, Harbiye, a popular local eatery. It was fascinating not just because of the attractive interior décor of hardwood, well-furnished fixtures, and a basic counter seating configuration; the same family had managed it since 1981. Their Fistikli kebap, or pistachio kebab, was out of this world. Another place I visited was the Asitane Restaurant, which warmed my heart with its magnificent lighting, large hanging images on the wall, and well-covered tables that offered a homey feel. The activity and beauty around Grand Bazaar are incomparable and a must-see attraction. It features the best products for shopping, including exquisite garments, silk, jewelry, fragrances, and pottery. Even though I had a lot of fun shopping, my favorite places to visit were the museums. These included the Istanbul Archaeological Museum, which had an amazing collection of artifacts from all over the world; the Museum of Natural History and Human Anatomy; and the Museum of Modern Art. After spending those precious days in Istanbul, now, when I look back on the days, it seems like a dream that came true; I still cannot believe that I walked through the alleys and the paths that have history embedded in them. Istanbul is a city with exquisite culture, trade, and a glorious past. Even today, more than ever, you can feel the heartbeat of a city by walking its streets.

SECTION II

12

CANADA

> *"...the most Canadian thing about Canada?*
> *The most Canadian thing about Canada is that when they ran a contest that went 'Finish this sentence.*
> *As American as apple pie.*
> *As Canadian as blank,' the winning answer was*
> *'As Canadian as possible under the circumstances'...."*
>
> — Margaret Atwood

Canada is the land of lakes and landscapes, maple and moose, bears and beers. God intentionally made Canada the second-largest country in the world; otherwise, there just wouldn't be enough space to fit all that beauty.

If you look out of any window in Canada, it will look like a painting waiting to be framed. Though the country is filled with maple trees, the streets of Canada smell like freshly brewed coffee. Every person you spot has a coffee-to-go in their hand, bustling down the road. Once you interact with them, you will realize why Canada is known for its politeness. Canadians are as sweet as their maple syrup!

Toronto:

Toronto is a city full of culture, art, and attractions. It is the perfect destination for a weekend getaway or a longer vacation. There is something for everyone in Toronto. Toronto is a beautiful and vibrant city that offers plenty of activities and attractions for tourists. One of the most significant attractions is hard to miss. The CN Tower offers amazing views of the city and is one of the tallest structures in the world.

CN Tower

Standing at a height of 1,815 feet, it is the tallest free-standing structure in the Western Hemisphere. The tower is a popular tourist destination, offering visitors stunning views of the city below.

It is also home to a number of restaurants. I would highly recommend the 360 Restaurant. The hotel rotates 360 degrees to offer visitors a panoramic view of the city. It is one of the most breathtaking sights even as your taste buds are entertained by the delicious fare served by the chef. I was shaken to my core by the view offered by the tower. CN Tower is one of the tallest towers in the world and the most popular tourist attraction in the city. Around 2 million tourists every year visit this site. CN stands for Canadian National, named after the railway company that built it.

The Royal Ontario Museum is a must-see for anyone interested in natural history and world cultures. It is one of the largest museums in North America. The museum is home to over six million artifacts from around the world, covering everything from ancient Egyptian mummies to dinosaurs to contemporary Canadian art. With such a vast and varied collection, there is something for everyone at the Royal Ontario Museum. The Royal Ontario Museum, also known as the ROM, has a collection of more than six million items. The museum draws more than one million visitors each year, making it the most popular museum in Canada. The museum was founded in 1912 and has since undergone several expansions. The most recent expansion was completed in 2016 and added an additional 30,000 square feet of exhibit space. The ROM is home to a diverse collection of art, culture, and natural history, with something to interest everyone.

The Royal Ontario Museum is home to many exhibits, but one of the most popular is the Egyptian Exhibit. This exhibit features many ancient artifacts from Egypt, as well as mummies and coffin displays. Visitors can learn about the ancient Egyptian culture and see some of the most famous artifacts in history. There is always something going on at the Royal Ontario Museum. They offer a variety of events that are sure to interest everyone. From art exhibits to educational programs, there is something for everyone at the Royal Ontario Museum. One of the most popular events is the Friday Night Live series. This is a program that offers live music, Toronto's best DJs, and light shows.

It is a great way to experience the museum after hours. Friday Night Live is a weekly event that offers visitors the opportunity to enjoy the museum after hours. The event includes live music, food and drink, and access to the museum's galleries and exhibits. Other popular events include family programs. These are designed to help families learn about different topics together. There are also a variety of workshops and classes offered at the Royal Ontario Museum. These are a great way to learn more about a certain topic or subject.

The Art Gallery of Ontario (AGO) is one of the largest art museums in North America. It has a collection of over 95,000 works of art. It was founded in 1900 and has a rich history of collecting and displaying art from around the world. In addition to its world-class permanent collection, the AGO also hosts a variety of temporary exhibitions throughout the year. It can be a treasure trove even if your preferences lie in classic art or contemporary art. The gallery has a variety of programs and events for visitors, including tours, workshops, and family-friendly activities. The gallery is also home to the AGO Art Rental and Sales program, which offers original works of art for rent or purchase. Visitors can also take advantage of the on-site cafe and shop, which make the perfect places to relax and take in the beauty of the Art Gallery of Ontario.

One of the more impressive sites in Toronto is the Ripley's Aquarium of Canada. This aquarium is home to over 16,000 aquatic animals and is one of the largest in North America. It is one of the top tourist destinations in Toronto. It is home to over 16,000 marine and freshwater animals from over 450 species. The Aquarium has 11 themed galleries, including the popular Canadian Waters Gallery, which is home to the world's second-largest freshwater aquarium. Visitors can explore different galleries, including the Canadian Waters Gallery, the Dangerous Lagoon, and the Tropical Rainforest Gallery. However, I was taken more by the state-of-the-art Aquarium Rescue Centre, where sick or injured animals are cared for by a team of veterinarians and aquarists. Rescued animals make up a large portion of the population and are an important part of the aquarium's mission.

The rescue team is on call 24 hours a day, 7 days a week to respond to calls about injured, orphaned, or abandoned wildlife. The animals that are brought to the aquarium are given a thorough examination by the veterinary team. They are then placed in quarantine until they are cleared to join the other animals on display. The aquarium has several large tanks that mimic natural habitats and provide the animals with plenty of space to swim and explore. The Aquarium's Animal Rescue Centre is equipped to handle any type of marine animal. The Centre has its own quarantine area, surgical suite, laboratory, and rehabilitation pool. The Centre also has a team of veterinarians, biologists, and certified rescue divers who are dedicated to rescuing and rehabilitating marine animals.

Canada also has many other stunning sightseeing sites. The parks can be like an oasis of calm amidst the urban sprawl. I particularly enjoyed my time at High Park and Bellwood Park. High Park is the largest park in Toronto and one of the most popular destinations for tourists and locals alike. I am not exaggerating when I say High Park is a hidden gem in Toronto. The park is over 400 hectares and also features a zoo, which is home to over 1,000 animals.

Toronto – a city of stunning parks

In the springtime, the park comes alive with over 1,000 varieties of tulips. The aptly named Tulip Festival is a popular event that draws visitors from all over. From late May to early June, the Sakura Matsuri Cherry Blossom Festival celebrates High Park's Japanese Cherry Tree collection. First opened to the public in 1876, it was one of the first municipally owned parks in North America. Today, High Park is home to many historical landmarks, including an authentic Japanese Tea House built in 1938.

While High Park is an oasis of nature, Bellwood Park is a magical place located in the heart of Toronto. The park was originally created as a place for the wealthy to escape the heat of the city. Over time, the park has been used for a variety of purposes, including a military encampment during World War I. Bellwood Park is a great place to relax, take a walk, and enjoy the beauty of nature. It is an oasis of humanity and nature. Even the greatest cynic will breathe a sigh of relief at the warmth and companionship displayed in this park.

The park is full of life, with people of all ages and backgrounds coming together to enjoy the beautiful space. There is a real sense of community in the park, and it's easy to strike up a conversation with someone new. The people of Bellwood Park are what make it such a special place. I was witness to this ambiance when we had lunch at the park. We received friendly smiles as we laid out our picnic blanket and unwrapped the lunch packed by our hotel. The scene seemed right out of Archie's comics as we had sandwiches in a park in the balmy weather. We made casual acquaintances with some of the people who had come out to have lunches for their own. It was a perfect day all around.

However, the most memorable experience in Toronto was that our stay coincided with the IIFA. The International Indian Film Academy Awards was held in Toronto that year. We stayed at the Fairmont Hotel. It was also the hotel of choice for many of the Bollywood superstars. I caught the glimpse of Shahrukh Khan. I did have the chance to meet him a couple of times later on in my life. But that was the first time I had come across many stars in their flesh. It was a surreal experience. But I experienced the most surreal event when my parents stepped out for a formal dinner. They were dressed to the nines and were suddenly surrounded by a group of fans. They saw my parents and assumed that they were Bollywood actors and asked them to pose for a few photographs and even asked them for their autographs. It is a memory that is often revisited with great mirth in my house.

Speaking of which, the Canadian film industry has also been in the news for the longest time. It is known to have produced many talents who are beloved across the world. The city is an optimal setting for cinematography and attracts filmmakers from all over the world. Tourism in Toronto certainly uplifts the city's economy by a magnitude. Toronto welcomes over 47 million tourists annually. Tourists have a wide range of activities to enjoy. They could range from markets comprising of locally sourced fresh fruits and vegetables to exceptionally well-curated malls and even a fashion district to please the shopaholics.

At the same time, foodies savor incredible meals from high-end restaurants. Toronto, like Birmingham in the UK, is an extension of Punjab. Indians indeed love Canada. Although Canada has a diverse population, it has recently seen a spike in the Indian population. Studies show that there has been a 105% increase in permanent Indian residents and a 127% increase in Indian students in Canada between the years 2016 and 2019. Indian students were the largest contributor to the rise in Indian immigrants to Canada. The majority of Canada's population is senior citizens. This is why Canada encourages youth around the world to move to their country, seeking employment and educational opportunities.[19]

It has worked out well as securing a Visa to the US has gotten tougher with time. This is especially true for young techies who receive plenty of opportunities as Toronto is the headquarters of many multinational tech companies ranging from Apple, Google, Asus, Intel, Microsoft, etc. The technological department is known

---

[19] https://www.forbes.com/sites/stuartanderson/2020/02/03/indians-immigrating-to-canada-at-an-astonishing-rate/

to contribute more than $52 billion annually to the city's economy.

The pages of history will show that post the World War, many immigrants from Europe settled in parts of Canada. Since Europe also ruled India at the time, Indians were part of the British settlement. Veterans from the British army arrived in Canada. The Indo-Canadian community consisted of Punjabi Hindus, Sikhs, and Muslims in those early days. Canada was a refuge for thousands of Indians who wanted to start a new life. About 1.4 million Canadians are indigenous people. At least 70,000 of them live in Toronto. The First Nation people, Metis, and Inuit are all part of this group.

The economy of Toronto began to take shape as the settlement in the Ontario province started developing. Toronto supplied essential goods to Ontario. Cities also relied on Toronto for transport as it acted as a railway junction. Due to the number of rivers in Toronto, the harbor was used frequently to ship goods. Currently, the rate has come down significantly.

Toronto is also an important financial hub. Bay Street in Toronto has the same reputation in Canada as Wall Street in New York. The city is also a base for all five of Canada's most important banks. The Toronto Stock Exchange ranks among the top five largest stock exchanges. Toronto is celebrated for its high-end restaurants that deliver and cater to various cuisines. With the rise in the Indian and the Indo-Canadian community, it was obvious that there would be demand for restaurants serving Indian food. Tandoori Flame is an Indian restaurant that can even beat Indian marriages in its plentiful array of food. With more than 150+ food items and its sumptuous meal, the place lures in people from all over the world. Indian food is omnipresent, but street food for meat lovers in the form of hot dogs and sausages can be equally exciting. The street food in Toronto offers a bite from many different cultures. At least once a day, while strolling in the streets of Toronto, you catch a whiff of pizza, the god of baked goods. I am a pizza lover. The Pineapple on Pizza or the Hawaiian Pizza, which originated in Ontario, has been a controversial topic. But I'm guilty of enjoying a good slice. Sorry, but not sorry!

Speaking of controversial but delicious dishes, one should also try 'The Persian.' There is an ongoing debate about whether it is a donut or cinnamon bun. It is topped with a secret pink icing that has been around for 70+ years. The icing is a tightly kept trade secret. You have to try it for yourself to discover the flavor. The place to try this famous dessert is Thunder Bay, and you cannot find this dessert anywhere else![20] A foodie's visit to Toronto is incomplete without trying their ever-popular butter tarts. I also got to sample the Macintosh Apples and Canada Dry Ginger Ale, a perfect drink if you want to avoid soda or if you are a teetotaller or underage for drinking alcohol.

Vancouver and British Colombia:

Our journey in Canada continued into Vancouver. We stayed in the Hotel Fairmont just as we did in Toronto. The stay was rejuvenating, but it was only a tiny part of a great trip. Canada's most densely populated city has more than 52% of people who are not native English speakers, which is evidence of its rich diversity. The two colors which dominate Vancouver are blue and green. Blue represents its ocean playgrounds, and green represents its vast green belt. We went to Victoria, British Columbia, a small town where one can walk and enjoy French cuisine. As you might have guessed, Victoria is named after Queen Victoria. The British colonized the area, and their settlement began as early as the 18th century. Victoria's eye-catching architecture can be credited to the famous architect, Rattenbury. He designed a few famous landmarks like the Parliament building, The Empress Hotel, Victorian Roedde House, and the Vancouver Art Gallery. Every stroll in the street is a museum-like experience in Victoria.[21]

---

[20] https://www.narcity.com/ontarios-secret-persian-dessert-has-been-hiding-from-the-rest-of-canada-and-its-delicious

[21] https://www.frommers.com/destinations/victoria/in-depth/art--architecture

One of the places we visited was Stanley Park. Vancouver is home to more than 10,000 indigenous people. Initially, Stanley Park was a settlement for indigenous people. But when the British colonized British Columbia, it became one of the most known parks in Vancouver. The forest atmosphere gives Stanley Park a different vibe compared to other modern parks. In addition, hundreds of species inhabit the park and make occasional appearances. The aquarium and other exhibits can be a fun experience. This visit to Stanley Park was followed by a visit to the Lions Gate Bridge, which is named after the two mountain peaks called the lions. It is a suspension bridge that can be thrilling or bile-inducing. I remember walking on it and it remains a fond memory. The bridge is quite high as it allows for cruise ships to pass under it. There is an observation deck called the Prospect Point that allows for a moment to just see this beautiful city framed with the Burrard Inlet and the mountains. I remember a few people squeaking in surprise as they looked down at the swathe of water. That particular view is not for the mild-hearted.

The Vancouver Aquarium is another site to experience nature. You can even see dolphins, sea lions, and whales at the Vancouver Aquarium. The aquarium is of great importance for maritime researchers and students. In addition, one must visit the Museum of Anthropology, a historic and contemporary native art center. I love swimming, and Vancouver housed Canada's longest pool. Even though I was young, I had an exhilarating experience there. It measures more than 400 feet deep and is nearly the size of three Olympic pools.

The Vancouver economy is funded by its big sea terminal. It also hosts a lot of cruise liners from LA to Alaska. The port brings home more than $172 billion in trade annually. Vancouver's houses range from long indigenous houses to suburban houses to modern and contemporary houses and apartments. It is said that Vancouver is one of the most expensive cities globally when it comes to affording a home. Vancouver, and particularly British Colombia, is linked to forest and fishery.

Vancouver Skyline

However, coal mining, lead mining, and gold mining began around 1846, allowing for a strong economic boost. Coal continues to be mined in tonnes.

In 2013, British Colombia produced 31 tonnes of coal, adding to Vancouver's reputation as the world's leading center for mineral exploration.[22]

The tourism industry in Vancouver is ever-thriving. The beauty of Vancouver, supported by the majestic views of water and mountains, adds scenic value to the tourism sector. This sector multiplies the city's economy as it provides jobs for more than 70,000 people.[23] Vancouver forms a rich cultural quotient for visitors with several museums, theatres, libraries, and festivals lined up.

---

[22] https://opentextbc.ca/geography/chapter/5-3-british-columbias-natural-resources/

[23] https://www.canada.ca/en/innovation-science-economic-development/news/2018/08/greater-vancouver-board-of-trade-meet-and-greet-exploring-opportunities-to-grow-bc-tourism.html

Vancouver is a hub for film and television production in Canada and offers a variety of tax incentives for productions. Vancouver's film tax credit program has been successful in attracting Hollywood productions to the city. The program provides a refund of up to 16% of eligible production costs, which makes Vancouver an attractive location for filmmakers.[24] In addition, Vancouver's diverse locations and scenery make it a desirable filming destination.

However, the greatest role that Vancouver plays is in Hollywood films. We have already established that Vancouver is a very diverse city. You may not have realized it, but some of your favorite movies use Vancouver to play different cities. Take, for example, the movie Mission Impossible: Ghost Protocol. The film is set in more than a few different settings. The story will take you to Seattle, Russia, Eastern Europe, Dubai, and even Mumbai. However, the filmmakers did not shoot any action sequences in Seattle, Eastern Europe, and Mumbai. These scenes were all shot in Vancouver. This is not the only movie to fake the setting and location in its story. The Seth Rogan and James Franco-starrer film, The Interview, has many scenes set in North Korea. Can you guess where they shot the North Korean scenes? Vancouver. I only realized this as I strolled through the city. Once you recognize the landmarks, you will know that you have been fooled. Much like how the Hollywood films use the stage to tell us so many memorable stories, Vancouver dons the guise of many a city in that storytelling process. It is the presence of such diverse views and generous tax credits that have seen filmmakers flock to this city.

Victoria Island

Victoria Island is a small island located in the British Columbia region of Canada. The island is home to a population of just over 4,000 people and is a popular tourist destination due to its natural

---

[24] https://www.vancouvereconomic.com/vancouver-film-commission/competitive-production-tax-credits/

beauty. Victoria Island is home to a number of beaches, hiking trails, and other outdoor attractions.

If you ever get the chance to visit Canada, make sure to have Victoria Island in your itinerary. You can pencil it in for a one-day trip or as a stopover. We went to the island via ship. It maintains the Victorian charm and you may feel like you have stepped into a weird time machine. The place boasts the mildest temperatures in the country and is dotted with gardens. I am not exaggerating when I say that it is one of the most beautiful cities in the world.

Victoria is a beautiful city with plenty to see and do. The Butchard Gardens, the Royal BC Museum, and the Art Gallery of Greater Victoria are all must-see places when visiting the city. Beacon Hill Park is a great place to take a stroll or have a picnic, and Craigdarroch Castle is a stunning example of Victorian architecture. It is a world-famous destination for gardeners and flower lovers. The Butchard Gardens, located in Brentwood Bay, is world-renowned for its display of flowers, plants, and shrubs.

The gardens feature over 55 acres of stunning floral displays, making it one of the largest and most beautiful gardens in Canada. Visitors can explore the gardens, take a nature walk, or enjoy a picnic lunch.

The Victoria General Hospital is another paradise for green thumbs. The hospital's rose garden is open to the public and features over 2,000 roses of all different varieties. The Royal BC Museum's botanical gardens feature a collection of over 3,000 different species of plants from British Columbia.

Another stunning sight is the Victoria Butterfly Gardens. It is the largest butterfly house in Canada and is home to over 3,000 butterflies from 50 different species. The gardens are a rainforest oasis and also feature a koi pond, waterfalls, and flowers. Visitors can learn about the life cycle of a butterfly, as well as the plants that they rely on for food. The gardens are open daily from 9:00 am to 5:00 pm. You could also take a boat tour for whale watching. You can sight orca, humpback whales, and bald eagles.

Craigdarroch Castle is a must-see for any history lover. The castle was built in the late 1800s by coal baron Robert Dunsmuir and is now a National Historic Site. The 19th-century Scottish Baronial mansion is one of the area's must-see places. The imposing structure was built by British Columbia's first governor, James Douglas, and is now a National Historic Site. Visitors can explore the mansion's grounds, which include a formal garden and a small cemetery, or take a guided tour of the house itself. While the mansion is perhaps most famous for its architecture, it also has a rich history, having been home to several generations of the Douglas family and playing host to some of British Columbia's most important political figures.

A food tour is a must-do in Victoria. You cannot miss Bannock Bread. The guide accompanying us on this tour explained that Scottish fur traders called *Selkirk* introduced *bannock* to the indigenous people of America over 200 years ago. The Scots cooked it in a griddle called a bannock stone, which they placed on the floor before a fire. (Picture can be added) One can visit many cafes on Lower Johnson Street (LoJo). The street is filled with craft breweries. Canada prides itself on its craft beers. We also took a short trip away from the city to visit the vineyards and cider orchards. That was the best decision we made during the journey as it was highly refreshing. We visited the popular *2% Jazz*, renowned for single-origin Americanos. They take pride in roasting their own beans. You can sense the aroma of freshly roasted beans from miles away! The coffee lovers here carry the same bearings and persona as wine tasters; they know the exact plot of land those beans come from.

We also had the delicious handmade Cornish pasty at the Victoria Pie Co. One can also try their spinach, feta, and tomato with deliciously crumbly pastry. They also had my favorite apple-blueberry chocolate cream pie. But keeping all of these dishes aside, I have to acknowledge the absolute must-have in Canada: *Poutine*. Poutine is a rib-sticking street-food dish. A bed of French fries swims in gravy and is topped with cheese curds. Potato *and* cheese in one dish! What's not to love about it? I also loved stumbling across the Chocolate Project during a walk. The store was a chocolate connoisseur's paradise.

I tried Crème Brulee and mussels here. I had never tried them before. When I saw the dish, I regretted my choice. It did not look that appetizing and I was unsure. However, when I took my first bite, I was enthralled. It was a reminder that the world always has something more to offer more than what it looks.

Whistler:

Whistler is a world-renowned ski resort in British Columbia, Canada, just north of Vancouver. With two massive mountains, a vibrant village, and countless activities, there is something for everyone in Whistler. From skiing and snowboarding to ziplining and bungee jumping, there is no shortage of adrenaline-pumping activities. And after a long day of adventure, there are plenty of places to relax and enjoy the views. Whether you're looking for a winter wonderland or a summer playground, Whistler is the perfect destination.

Whistler is the best place to ski in Canada because of the snow. The snow is so powdery and light that it feels like you're skiing on clouds. It's also very consistent; you can usually count on there being fresh powder every day. And because it's so high up, the views are incredible. You really feel like you're in another world when you're skiing in Whistler.

Whistler is consistently ranked as one of the top ski destinations in the world and for good reason. The mountains are incredible with over 8000 acres of skiable terrain, 200+ marked trails, and 53 lifts. But it's not just the size that makes Whistler amazing, it's also the variety.

There is something for everyone with easy greens, challenging blacks, and everything in between. The views from the top of the mountains are stunning and there is always a great atmosphere on the slopes.

Whistler is set against a stunning backdrop of tall mountain peaks and lush greenery, making it one of the most beautiful places to ski in Canada. The resort town is also home to a variety of shops, restaurants, and bars, as well as a lively nightlife scene, so there's plenty to keep you entertained off the slopes.

Whistler

Whistler is also one of the best places in North America to watch bears. There are three species of bears that can be found in Whistler: black bears, grizzly bears, and polar bears. Black bears are the most common and can be found in both the valley and the mountains. Grizzly bears are less common but can be found in both the valley and the mountains. Polar bears are the rarest, and can only be found in the mountains.

Bear watching is an amazing experience that everyone should have at least once in their life. Whistler is the perfect place to do it, and with a little planning, you can have an unforgettable time. First, research what time of year is best for bear-watching in Whistler. This will ensure that you see the most bears possible.

Second, make sure to book a tour with a reputable company. This will give you the best chance of seeing bears and staying safe. Finally, don't forget to bring your camera! (The last tip is to highlight my chagrin as we forgot to take the camera on our trip!) Thus, the first activity we did in Whistler was to take up a guided back bear viewing tour. It was an exhilarating experience to spot the giant bears right in front of our eyes. No picture or video can ever truly capture the size and majesty of these beasts. Even though we didn't have a camera on us to capture the moment, the experience is forever etched in our minds.

Whistler is a municipality resort that benefits mainly from tourism. The special quality of Whistler is that it not only attracts global tourists but retains them and urges them to visit at least a few more times.

It is also ranked as the number one ski resort in the world. Whistler offers luxury in a way you've never perceived before. We took the gondola to the top of the ski slopes. The gondola is a means of transport for the people who want to ski and for a gorgeous view for the tourists. I was also lucky that my father booked the helicopter tour of Whistler, and we got clear skies. It is a half-hour tour that will just take your breath away and leave you shaken in a good way. It can be a spiritual experience. We could fly through 12000-year-old glaciers, and you get to land on one if you are lucky. We were. Although we had to rush back in 10-15 minutes, I have never experienced something more sensational in my life. The feeling of standing on top of a glacier as you felt it creakily move is unparalleled.

While Canada does leave such lasting impressions, I cannot but forget one traumatic impression. My trip was marred by Stanley cup riots. Some of the window panes outside our hotel were broken and shops were closed. Canada is a peaceful country and the Canadians I met were extremely sweet and polite. Perhaps it is why those riots remain a shocking memory. Violence of any kind must be avoided and if it is especially related to sports, it would be best to steer clear of it. There are plenty of reasons to visit Canada – it's a beautiful country with plenty to see and do.

The scenery is breathtaking. From the rocky mountains to the lush forests, Canada is home to some of the most stunning landscapes in the world. The people are friendly and welcoming. Canadians are known for their warmth and hospitality, so you're sure to feel right at home. The balmy summers will feel just like home for any North Indian. They have some of the most delectable cuisines from French, British and Indian representation. It may not be as industrialized and urban as it is neighbor, the USA. However, therein lies the charm of this easy-paced, polite, and warm country.

13

USA

"When I was growing up, I don't remember being told that America was created so that everyone could get rich. I remember being told it was about opportunity and the pursuit of happiness. Not happiness itself, but the pursuit."—Martin Scorsese#

I love the USA because it is the land of the dreams. It is the land of opportunities. I am sure many have heard these words. However, it is not just about the words. I can say that it goes beyond any marketing spin. There is an attitude, a mindset that makes this country special. The possibilities are infinite. The next millionaire could be staying across your room. It is the land of dreamers and doers. It is the land of millionaires, entrepreneurs, and millions of students from all over the world. They are all pursuing the American Dream. When you visit the US, you cannot help but visualize living there. You see a future and the US has everything to make it come true. All you need is a dream and the desire to achieve it. There is no better embodiment of this idea than New York. It is the city that never sleeps.

Think of any sprawling urban landscape. What will you think of? What images will your imagination show you? I can tell you what popular culture might show you. It will be buildings reaching out to the sky as they become visible from the enshrouded morning fog. There will be huge suspension bridges steeped in history. It will have character. There will be museums, cultural centers, and other famous places. Crucially, there will be a sense of pride among its residents. New York is all that and more. When you land in New York, you will know that you have come to a special place. The air itself is charged with it.

New York Skyline

It is a fantastically glorious city with equally mythical lore. It was the center of the mafia culture with iconic figures immortalized in infamy. If you were to notice it, you will find there New York is a place full of personalities. New Yorkers have the gift of gab. Perhaps it is this trait that has seen New York become the media capital of the world. Los Angeles may have the famed Hollywood film studios, but New York is home to the top news organizations, magazines, and book publishers in the world. The city also has a large number of advertising, public relations, and media relations firms. New York is also the home of the major broadcast networks, cable channels, and movie studios. It is home to some of the biggest media companies in the world. These companies include but are not limited to, Time Warner, News Corp, CBS, and ABC. New York is also home to many smaller media companies and organizations. The media presence in New York is unrivaled by any other city in the world.

The media landscape in New York is constantly changing and evolving. New media companies are always popping up and established companies are always expanding their operations. This makes New York an exciting place for anyone interested in the media. There are always new opportunities and new challenges to be faced. The city's media outlets include some of the most prestigious and influential newspapers, magazines, television networks, and digital media companies in the world. New York is also home to a vibrant and diverse community of media professionals, including journalists, editors, producers, and other creative professionals. It remains at the forefront of innovation in the media industry. In recent years, New York has seen a surge in new media startups, as well as continued growth in traditional media companies. The city is also home to a number of major media trade shows and conferences, including the New York Media Festival and the International Consumer Electronics. New York is the media capital of the world because it is home to the biggest and most influential media companies. Many of these companies are headquartered in New York City, and they have a major presence in the city.

New York is suffused with a mentality of achievement and endeavor. One cannot help but think of Frank Sinatra and how the vagabond shoes want to stray into the heart of the city. Frank Sinatra's song *New York, New York* talks of how if you can make it in New York means you can make it anywhere. There has to be some truth to that statement. If you were to look at the music industry, it was New York that witnessed how punk music became mainstream in the 80s when the CBGB bar gave a stage to some of the upcoming bands.

The bar which began as a place for musicians who catered to Country, Bluegrass, and Blues genres of music would become the mecca for punk music. Some of the most iconic musical acts like Talking Heads, Blondie, Television, The Police, the Ramones, and Patti Smith all found their voice at CBGB in New York.

The city, however, is not just about the gab; it is also about the jab. There is a reason why Dana White pursued the cause of the Ultimate Fighting Championship (UFC) to host an event in New York. New York has the famed Madison Square Garden which has hosted some of the most iconic boxing fights. Dana White needed the UFC in New York to gain legitimacy for his mixed martial arts promotion. No other city in the world had that aura to provide.

Madison Square Garden is one of the most iconic venues in the world and has been home to some of the most legendary moments in sports and entertainment history. Today, it remains one of the busiest arenas in the world, hosting hundreds of events each year. The current Garden is the fourth venue to bear the name Madison Square Garden. The first two were located on Madison Avenue and 26th Street, with the third Madison Square Garden (now demolished) further uptown at Eighth Avenue. The Garden is currently used to regularly host professional basketball and ice hockey games. It also hosts concerts, boxing, circuses, ice shows, professional wrestling, and many sports and entertainment events.

In 1879, P.T. Barnum's "Greatest Show on Earth" circus opened in Madison Square, and the area became a popular entertainment destination. The circus was so successful that it set the stage for more stage shows and events at the Garden. One of the most famous and successful stages shows at Madison Square Garden was the Ziegfeld Follies. The Follies were a series of elaborate musical theatrical acts that featured the most beautiful and talented performers of the time. The Follies were so popular that they helped make Madison Square Garden one of the most famous venues in the world. Madison Square Garden has been the home of some of the most iconic moments in sports and entertainment history. From the "Miracle on Ice" at the 1980 Winter Olympics to Muhammad Ali's legendary boxing matches, the "World's Most Famous Arena" has seen it all.

According to a study conducted by the American Gaming Association, the Garden generates $1.2 billion in annual economic activity for the city. This includes $600 million in direct spending by visitors and $600 million in indirect spending related to things like transportation and hotels. In total, the Garden supports 4,800 jobs in the city.

New York City is an amazing place full of life and adventure. There is always something to do, whether you're exploring the sights and sounds of Times Square or taking in the views from the top of the Empire State Building. And with so many different neighborhoods to discover, you are sure to find one that suits your style.

There are five boroughs in New York City. They are the Bronx, Brooklyn, Manhattan, Queens, and Staten Island. I found each borough is unique and with its own culture and history. The Bronx is known for its hip-hop culture. It is the northernmost borough. It is the only borough that is located on the mainland of the United States. It is home to the Yankee Stadium, the Bronx Zoo, and the New York Botanical Garden.

Brooklyn is the most populous borough, with over 2.6 million residents. I found some iconic landmarks like the Brooklyn Bridge and Coney Island in this borough. I also found the borough to be a fertile ground for creative expression with its vibrant arts scene and hipster culture.

Manhattan is where I felt my connection. It was as if a hermit crab had found its new shell. Manhattan is the financial and business center of New York City. It is the most well-known and densely populated borough of New York City. I found many iconic landmarks and attractions, including Times Square, Central Park, and the Empire State Building here. As I explored it further, I came to realize that Manhattan was divided into three main sections: Lower, Midtown, and Upper Manhattan. Lower Manhattan is home to the Financial District and Battery Park, while Midtown is home to Times Square and the Rockefeller Center. Upper Manhattan is home to Harlem.

Queens is where I found the most ethnically diverse populace. From the hipster enclaves of Astoria to the immigrant communities of Flushing and Jackson Heights, Queens had something worth exploring. It is home to some of New York's most iconic attractions, including Citi Field, the home of the Mets; Flushing Meadows-Corona Park, site of the US Open Tennis tournament; and Queens Museum. I also found that the diversity of this borough was not limited to its populace. It also extended to its culinary outlets. I found a wealth of great dining options, from street food to Michelin-starred restaurants.

Staten Island is the least populated borough but is home to the Staten Island Ferry, which provides views of the Statue of Liberty. It is the southernmost borough and is home to the Statue of Liberty. It is quite unmissable. I have always associated the US with the Statue of Liberty. It is a massive monument and I could see it from my flight as were landing at John F Kennedy International Airport. While we have come to think of the statue as American, history will reveal that it was a gift from the French to the United States to mark their independence. A French sculptor *Frédéric Auguste Bartholdi* was the creator of this iconic statue, which is now America's biggest tourist attraction.

When we landed in New York, my uncle came and whisked us away to his home at Long Island. The first thing that I noticed was the traffic. The vehicles stuck to the right-hand side of the road. This can be challenging to an Indian who has only known traffic to flow on the left-hand side of the road. Maybe it was the strangeness that I, without realizing it, opened the left side front door of the car. As I looked, I was surprised to see the steering wheel. It was a source of great laughter for my uncle and parents. I rushed to the other side and opened the door and screamed as they do in the movies, "Shotgun!" Even as my uncle drove, the entire experience seemed weird. I was seemingly on the wrong side, and everything seemed inverted. However, it did seem fun and it never got old during my stay there.

Statue of Liberty

The first place I saw was America's most iconic sight, the Statue of Liberty. The Statue of Liberty should be on every visitor's list regardless of their schedule. I know it may sound a little clichéd, but you will agree with me once you see it for yourself. The view of the Statue of Liberty, even from far away, can be enthralling. As we prepared to leave my uncle's house, my aunt gave me an ear muzzle. I wondered why, but that question was answered as we traveled by car to the ferry. We were buffeted by strong winds and rain. We took the boat trip to see the Statue of Liberty at close quarters. Unfortunately for us, New York's weather was determined to create difficulties. We braved the rain with our uncontrollable umbrellas. Yet, it was worth it in the end.

There are many amazing places to visit in New York City, but one of the most amazing is Central Park. Central Park is a large park in the middle of the city that is a great place to relax, take a walk, or have a picnic.

There are also many events that take place in Central Park, such as concerts and festivals. There are also a number of famous landmarks within the park, including the Bethesda Fountain and the Belvedere Castle. Though it is not the largest park in New York, it is definitely the more popular one. Central Park was created in the years 1857-1876.

The population of New York started multiplying in force. The people of Manhattan were drawn to open spaces away from the rush and business of the city area. Soon enough, there was a public demand for a park, and after weighing the pros and cons, the New York City Council decided to go for it. The park now comprises several attractions, most of which can be availed free of cost. Hence, one of the budget-friendly things one can do in the city is to visit the park. The walk and a carriage ride that takes you through the crisscrossing pathways of the Central are delightful experiences.

The Empire State Building is one of the most recognizable buildings in the world. Located in Midtown Manhattan, the Empire State Building offers stunning views of the city from its observation decks. The views from the top are incredible and you can see for miles.

After the tragic 9/11 terrorist attacks, it became the tallest building in the city. However, 9/11 is such a poignant moment in New York's history. One should take the time to visit Ground Zero.

The site of the former World Trade Center is now home to the National September 11 Memorial and Museum. The memorial features two massive waterfalls and reflecting pools, surrounded by the names of the victims of the 9/11 attacks. The museum tells the story of the attacks and their aftermath through artifacts, photos, and personal accounts. Ground Zero is a powerful reminder of the tragedy of 9/11 and its impact on New York City and the world. It is also a place that reflects the grit and never-say-die attitude of New Yorkers.

Another iconic site is Times Square. It is a major commercial and entertainment hub, as well as a symbol of the city. It is always bustling with activity and has a wide variety of attractions, including theaters, restaurants, shops, and more. Times Square is also home to the world-famous New Year's Eve ball drop. Given my interest in commerce, I was bedazzled by Wall Street.

It is a place that's steeped in history. This is where the financial industry began, and it's still an important part of the city's economy. You can see the New York Stock Exchange, the Federal Reserve Bank of New York, and a variety of other financial institutions. It is home to the headquarters of 65 Fortune 500 companies including, Verizon, JP Morgan Chase, and Citigroup. One of the more popular and iconic sights here is that of the Charging Bull. The bronze sculpture was installed by Arturo Di Modica after the 1987 Wall Street crash. It reflects the courage of New Yorkers. Unlike other attractions, the bull is not ticketed. So there are a lot of people who wish to take photos with it. If you are among them, do not be surprised if it takes you 30 minutes to get one.

One of the most popular places to visit is the Rockefeller Center. This world-famous complex is home to NBC Studios, the Top of the Rock Observation Deck, and many other attractions. However, when it comes to shopping, do not look any further than Fifth Avenue.

There are a number of high-end shops that line the street. Fifth Avenue is also home to the New York Public Library and some of the best museums in the city.

Straddling the east river is the famous Brooklyn Bridge. The suspension bridge with neo-gothic themed arches and cables is one of the more recognizable bridges in the world. Originally it was supposed to connect Brooklyn and New York (Manhattan), then regarded as two independent cities. They had to consider building the bridge as the ferry lines were the only available and active mode of transportation. However, the ferries can only transport a minuscule amount of people compared to the people who wanted to travel between the two points. Several options were considered including building tunnels under the river. However, the council chose to build the Brooklyn bridge considering the prohibitive financial costs of the other options.

The bridge was not inexpensive either. It cost the two cities over $15M to build the bridge, but it was easily recovered by the tolls that were collected initially. The bridge boosted Brooklyn's population as there was now a way to commute to their jobs and other commitments in New York.

The bridge spanning over 272 ft in height also allows ships and boats to commute easily under it. However, the bridge also marks the optimism of architects and engineers toward technology. However, such progressive bridges were not very common back then; the locals doubted its stability. It is said that a circus showman walked 21 elephants on the bridge to prove its stability. Though the bridge was created to connect the two towns, it grew to become a popular symbol of New York.[25]

Another sight very commonly associated with NYC is the skyline filled with skyscrapers. The current architectural outlook of New York City with many high-rise establishments was primarily influenced by the City's economic development, especially over the past century.

The city utilized ideologies from all over the world, evolving from a Dutch fur-trading center to a global business destination where German and Jewish builders constructed most of the tenement buildings in New York. They did this due to their primal(?) culture in curating architecture and designs. An example is the German Detlef Lienau, who commissioned the DeLancey Kane Estate loft building and the original Brooklyn Academy of Music. Major city infrastructures were built or renovated and restored, including the Chrysler building, designed by Walter Chrysler and unveiled in his Art Deco in 1930. Walter Chrysler's Art Deco design is among the most prolific architectural designs that define New York City and showcases its prominence in the last two centuries. The high-rise trend is expected to continue as the city reinvents its urban spaces through new landmarks and tall residential buildings.

New York's economy is unquestionably thriving as it is

---

[25]http://www.brooklynbridgeaworldwonder.com/economic-effect.html

considered the top destination for business and commerce. New York's economic value competes almost equally with that of Canada's. New York's GDP was evaluated to be $1.9 Trillion in the year 2021, ranking just below California and Texas. However, it is all set to surpass Tokyo by 2035. NYC is indeed just 1% of the gigantic US. However, no genre of business is missed out on NYC's list. It has been the hub for transport, trade, fashion, media, real estate, legal service, theatre, art, etc.

The biggest Fortune 500 companies are headquartered in New York. It is also a fulcrum of the entrepreneurial community, so it is no surprise that New York is home to the greatest number of billionaires.

The Financial Industry of the US, better known as Wall Street, is also headquartered in New York. The name originates from the wall the Dutch built to keep the British and the pirates out. The wall was demolished long ago, but the name stayed on. It was originally called de Waalstraat in Dutch and was used as a marketplace to trade slaves and securities. In the 19th century, many businesses settled down in the city. In a way, the American street has always been utilized commercially.

Initially, independent brokerage firms presided over Wall Street. But now, numerous banks and parties have taken an interest in the financial industry of the U.S. If you do not believe me, I recommend reading up on the case of Gamespot. The U.S is the world's biggest contributor to the global economy, and that status is no joke. It produces almost double the GDP of China ($16.44 trillion), with a GDP of $22.68 trillion in 2021. Since Wall Street is majorly responsible for the U.S economy, it also influences the global economy. We saw it play out with the financial markets crash in 2008.

New York City is widely known for its diversity and acceptance. Its economic growth attracted Irish, Jews, and Italian immigrants to the city. The steady growth of Wall Street opened up employment options and invited thousands of immigrants to settle in NYC. These factors have transformed New York's cultural Image. High rates of immigration promoted a population boost crowning New York as America's largest city. As communities started to form in New York, the city became more hospitable. People of different ethnicities began to follow in the footsteps of those successful in New York.

The cabs of New York are impossible to miss. Anyone who has traveled to New York has experienced the subtle privilege of a cab service. Before Lyft and Uber took over, the yellow cab service was quite popular in New York. As you would have seen in many films with NYC as a setting, the streets were filled with yellow cars like bees in a hive.

It was during the time of the great depression that unemployed men turned to taxi services for generating income. The streets of New York burst with taxis almost overnight. The city is said to have employed 82% of immigrants as cabbies. This is the unbreakable spirit of New York. Its residents swear by it.

New York has more than 3500 coffeehouses. Coffee and sugar are intimately bound up with New York history. Even Starbucks, the mega-brand, began in this city. The first New York stock exchange business was conducted in Tontine Coffee House. While learning more about Coffee and New York, I came across an excerpt written by a gentleman from England who visited the Tontine Coffee House.

Excerpt:

The Tontine coffee-house was filled with underwriters, brokers, merchants, traders and politicians; selling, purchasing, trafficking, or insuring; some reading, others eagerly inquiring the news. The steps and balcony of the coffee-house were crowded with people bidding or listening to several auctioneers, who had elevated themselves upon a hogshead of sugar, a puncheon of rum or a bale of cotton; with Stentorian voices were exclaiming "Once. Twice." "Once. Twice." "Thank ye, gentlemen." Or were knocking down the goods which took up one side of the street to the best purchaser. The coffee-house slip, and the corners of Wall and Pearl-streets, were jammed up with carts, drays, and wheelbarrows; horses and men were huddled promiscuously together, leaving little or no room for passengers to pass.[26]

Coffee has a significant impact on the architecture of the city. In the 19th Century, the US loved coffee so much that it accounted for half of the worldwide consumption of it. The Revolutionary War, while being an important historical period, influenced the urban city plan of New York. Due to the war, sugar had to be channeled within the US. So New York became a manufacturing city. Today, you can see how the city's urban layout incorporates these centuries-old factories and mills. These developments also defined the culture of local populations. 19% of workers employed in NYC worked in the sugar refining industry.

It is a mark of the multicultural nature that the falafel and the BEC seemed to be the leading local foods I experienced in New York. The falafel appeared to be a favorite among the locals. Falafel is made from a blend of ground chickpeas and herbs, fried like a cake and served with tahini, ground sesame seeds emulsified with a bit of oil, and fresh vegetables. It also aligns with the fast-paced life of the city. I love Falafel, and it became my go-to food during the trip. The best place to have falafel in NYC is Mamoun's Falafel, the oldest falafel restaurant in the city.

Another fantastic place we discovered in our food hunt is Milk N' Honey. Liebman's Kosher Deli is a great food place. We had a breaded chicken sandwich and a plain knish. The sandwich was quite plain for an Indian taste palate. I would have loved more seasoning. However, the knish was so well made! A knish is a Jewish snack. It is a round dough ball with a filling inside. Typically, potatoes are used. We also loved the potato pancake and coleslaw. New York also has a distinct pizza culture. There are pizzerias that serve the traditional Italian way and then there are the renegades. You will find people experimenting with different toppings like poke and ramen. Then there are pizzerias that serve you pizzas with a cauliflower base. If you are really up for it, Wall Street has the Industry Kitchen which

---

[26] https://www.6sqft.com/roasteries-and-refineries-the-history-of-sugar-and-coffee-in-nyc/

will serve you the most indulgent 24k pizza. It is a $2000 pizza with toppings of truffles, foie gras, caviar, and gold.

The Italian migrants brought the pizza. However, there is one particular dish that cannot be separated from New York, the hamburger. In the early 1900s, New York was home to a thriving burger scene. German immigrants had brought over the hamburger and it quickly caught on with the city's residents. By the 1920s, there were hundreds of burger joints in New York, each with its own unique take on the classic sandwich. It was during this time that the hamburger began to be seen as an American icon. New Yorkers were proud of their burger joints and would often recommend them to out-of-towners. This helped to spread the popularity of the hamburger outside of New York, and by the 1930s, it was a national phenomenon. Today, the hamburger is one of America's most beloved foods, and it has its roots in New York.

New York may be known for its hot dogs and pizza, but that doesn't mean its burger culture should be overlooked. Some of the best burger joints in the city can be found in Manhattan, Queens, and Brooklyn. Whether you're looking for a classic burger with all the fixings or something more unique, you're sure to find something to your taste.

One of the best places to get a burger in New York is Shake Shack. Shake Shack is considered a New York institution. Shake Shack is a chain that started in New York, and they make some of the best burgers in the city. While they are more famous for their burgers made with 100% all-natural Angus beef, we opted for the Chick'n ShackBurger. They are cooked to perfection. They also offer a variety of other menu items, including hot dogs, shakes, and salads.

PYT is a burger joint in New York City that is known for its unique and over-the-top burgers. The restaurant has been featured on many food shows and has been acclaimed by many food critics. The menu features a wide variety of burgers, all of which are made with fresh, local ingredients. The burgers are cooked to order and can be customized to your liking. The restaurant also offers a wide selection of sides, including fries, onion rings, and salads.

If you want a good burger in New York City, you can't go wrong with Five Guys. The burgers are juicy and flavorful, and the fries are some of the best around. The only downside is that the line can get pretty long, especially during peak hours.

There are a lot of burger joints in New York City, but The Counter is one of the best. They have a great selection of burgers, including veggie burgers, and the fries are some of the best in the city. BurgerFi is another famous burger chain that started in New York City. The chain is known for its fresh, made-to-order burgers and fries. BurgerFi also has a unique selection of toppings, including avocado, bacon, and even fried eggs. There are an endless amount of burger joints in New York City, but only a few can make the top ten list. Corner Bistro is a burger lover's dream come true. With its classic American food and perfect fries, it is no wonder that this is one of the most popular burger places in the city. The Bistro also offers a great selection of beer, making it the perfect place to watch a game or grab a quick bite with friends.

However, the outstanding cuisine experience was when we visited Devi. It is a Michelin-star restaurant run by chefs Suvir and Hemant. They are a legendary pair as they earned the first Michelin star at Devi for not just Indian but also any non-North European restaurant in North America in 2007. It happens to be one of the more defining Indian food experiences in India and abroad. I would highly recommend their chicken masala. It is absolutely lip-smacking.

Niagara Falls

I would be remiss to not mention Niagara Falls when I talk of New York. The Niagara Falls is a group of three waterfalls: The Horseshoe Falls, American Falls, and the Bridal Veil Falls. The latter two lies in the United States and the first one straddles the international border between the United States and Canada. The US border falls in the New York state. It is a phenomenal state. You can hear the roar of the water and then you can see the curtains of mist rising from the water crashing down. Then you see the majesty of the waterfalls. The two best ways to experience the might and majesty of the waterfalls are the Maid of the Mist boat tour and the Cave of Winds. The first is a boat ride which will take you around the falls and you will be hit with the sheets of the mists of water. The second is a set of wooden walkways that lead you right next to the Bridal Veil waterfall. These walkaways are reconstructed every year. When I walked up to that spot, I was sprayed with water. I could not help but marvel at the how nature could be brutal, majestic, and beautiful at the same time.

Maid of the Mist boat tour

FLORIDA

From New York, we then visited Orlando. It is home to the world-famous Disneyland. We spent five days in Orlando and stayed at the Hyatt, a massive resort hotel. However, we did not have the time to explore the many delights of the place as I was entranced by Disneyland. We spent most of the five days on Disney tours. I had been to the Disneyland in Hong Kong. But the American experience was something else. The scale was incomparably massive. It was also distinctly American in the snacks and food available.

There were the American diner staples like fries, corn, burgers, hot dogs, coke, etc. There was also the change that I was a bit older than when I visited the Hong Kong theme park. I was no longer restricted by my height.

Orlando Disneyland is one of the most popular tourist destinations in the world. Every year, millions of people flock to the park to experience the magic of Disney. From the moment you step through the gates, you are transported into a world of make-believe, where anything is possible. Whether you are young or old, there is something for everyone at Orlando Disneyland. From the thrill of the rides to the classic Disney characters, there is something for everyone to enjoy.

My personal favorite was the Magic Kingdom and Hollywood Studios. Magic Kingdom is the most iconic part of Orlando Disneyland and is a must-see. There are plenty of classic rides, such as "It's a Small World" and the "Pirates of the Caribbean," as well as newer attractions like "Avatar Flight of Passage." If you love adventure, then the choice is easy – the Universal's Islands of Adventure. This park also houses the iconic Hogwarts castle from The Wizarding World of Harry Potter! It has some must-try butterbeer, the iconic drink from that magical world. A word of advice, buy the fresh one. The bottled ones do not taste the same. It also features attractions like Harry Potter and the Forbidden Journey and Hagrid's Magical Creatures.

Another equally stunning sight would be Animal Kingdom. As its name implies, Animal Kingdom is home to animals from all over the world. You can see elephants, tigers, cougars and hyenas among others. It is probably the biggest attraction in the entire park but it did not enchant me as much as I am a bit squeaky around reptiles. Epcot is a unique part of Orlando Disneyland that combines education with entertainment. There are pavilions devoted to different countries, as well as attractions like "Spaceship Earth" and "Test Track." For the souvenir hunters, there is no better place than Disney Springs. It is a shopping and dining area that offers a variety of plants and decorations from around the world. You can buy unique gifts for family and friends, as well as reloadable cards for museum-quality photography.

It is said that one must visit Disney three times in one's life:

1. When you are crazy about Mickey - which I did when I went to Hong Kong.
2. When you are crazy about thrills and Hollywood - which was part of my Orlando trip.
3. When you want to eat, party, and have fun; you go to a place like Epcot. It is part of my dream to do so when I grow up.

The parks are massive and you will have to walk a lot. Another word of advice would be to keep yourselves hydrated as it is also quite a humid place. We were there for five days and yet I must say we could have only explored about 60% of what Disneyland could offer.

There's no place like America! It is a land of enterprise and entertainment. From the hustle and bustle of New York City to the parks of Florida, there's something for everyone in America. There are many more wonders to be unfurled and I hope to do that sooner than later.

SECTION III

14

DUBAI

"Just a young gun with a quick fuse
I was uptight, wanna let loose
I was dreaming of bigger things
And wanna leave my old life behind
Not a yes-sir, not a follower
Fit the box, fit the mold
Have a seat in the foyer, take a number
I was lightning before the thunder."

If you are a music buff, I am sure you have heard the song *Thunder* by Imagine Dragons. The song has a music video with close to 2 billion views on YouTube. It has quite the arresting visuals with brilliant props and dance moves by the artists in the video. However, if you look closely at the video, you will see some majestic towers of glass and concrete. There are buildings that seem to dare to touch the sky. The city of Dubai is like the song lyrics and how it appears in the video. It is not a follower, or a fit the box, or a fit the mold type of city. It springs like a man-made monstrosity of a city oasis amidst the natural monstrosity of the desert that surrounds it.

When I first heard the song, I hummed and nodded my head to the beat and lyrics. However, when I saw the video, I was immediately transported back to the memories of my time in Dubai. Oh, what an exceptional experience it was! I am sure you have seen brochures of apartments that show exceptionally designed homes. If they make a brochure for cities, Dubai would be the advertisement. The roads are neat and orderly. The city was spic and span. However, it is not just about the geometric, architectural, and construction aesthetics that set Dubai apart. It is unique because of the way they embrace technology to counter the challenges set by the surrounding terrain.

Dubai has been named the most 'Environmentally Safe City' by the Kuwait-based Arab Towns Organisation. It based its decision on the city's track record in establishing efficient programs to keep the city clean and manage noise pollution and other pollutants. When I set foot in Dubai, I felt as if I was the kid who stumbled onto a carpet and a disused lamp. I was in awe, looking at the ostentatious land, the pomp, the opulence, and the grandeur that engulfed it. Well, in the case of Dubai, all the glitters can be gold; my friend jokingly told me so, but when I landed here, I came to know that the statement was a little more grounded in truth than humor.

In my mind, I have always associated the Middle East with oil and conservative culture as I had learned so from books, but little did I know that I was about to encounter a trip full of joy. Dubai can be an adventure for food lovers and shopaholics.

The Palm Jumeriah is composed of many beautiful luxury hotels and each of them offers all the amenities you would expect from a modern five-star property. It is also one of the iconic works that make Dubai a place of challenges. It is a place filled with humanity's affronts to nature as if to say I will do something extraordinary here. None embodies this more than the Palm Islands. These formations, visible from space, were created from sand dredged from the shallow waters of the Persian Gulf. There are very few man-made creations that are visible from space. An often-cited example is China's Great Wall, the only man-made creation visible from space.

However, a few more places can be sighted from space. One of them is the Palm Islands of Dubai. These islands were created from sand being dredged from the shallow waters of the Persian Gulf. People on the ground, using shovels, moved the sand into place to create the desired shape. If we were to liken it to a more simplistic process, it would be akin to creating stone steps in a park. The fabrication of the Palm Islands was an intensive process. One of the formations of the Palm Islands is Palm Jumeirah. It is an archipelago shaped like a palm tree. It is estimated that it cost $ 12 billion to construct it. This is not a project that many countries can undertake. Saudi Arabia is one of the few that can afford to undertake a project of this scale. So, they chose their capital city, Dubai, to be the site of this modern-day marvel. It was part of a stunning transformation of a city once a small fishing village in the 18th century. I am not a history buff, but I was curious to know the history of this lavish land to satisfy my quest to see the place's present-day commerce. I teleported myself back to the past (Ah! Only if I could go back to it in real, but I did so through the pages of a magazine that talked about the great ancient past that resulted in today's glamour of Dubai).

I glanced through the pages and realized that the commercial history of this place could be traced back to the early 20th century. Tourism began to develop as a significant source of income for the desert city. This was largely because of the pioneering work of one man, initially involved in the export of dates and then, subsequently, in that of expensive spices. After constructing hotels and restaurants at affordable prices, Charles de Gaulle, who later became France's leader during World War II, attracted many visitors to Dubai. According to historical records, Dubai was a walled city in the early 1800s. Around the same time that Dubai became a dependency, the Al Fahidi Fort was erected. On the Bur Dubai side, the wall ran from Al Fahidi Historical Neighbourhood through Al Fahidi Fort and stopped at the Old Souk. Al Ras was also walled off on the Deira side. However, in 1820, Britain established a maritime ceasefire with local authorities, ensuring that trade routes remained open and businesses could flourish.

With this came a regular engagement with nations from all over the world, establishing Dubai as a hub of vital activity.

However, being a traveler in this 21st century, my gaze cannot help but be captured by the skyscrapers and the pomp and gorgeous, gleaming city around me. There are perhaps no words that will do justice to the feelings I felt. There is no disputing that Dubai's skyscrapers are magnificent individually, but one lone, unbelievably towering structure stands sentry above them all, calmly observing the bustling metropolis at its feet. If you'd seen my exhilaration at the possibility of climbing the Burj Khalifa, the world's highest structure, you might have doubted my sanity.

And what a sight it is, gleaming in the early sun against a deep blue sky with only a sprinkling of white, wispy clouds fluttering by. It took six years to construct, and it was completed in 2010. It is another testament to how Dubai is filled with landmarks challenging nature. Burj Khalifa seems like an effort to pierce the heavens and is a remarkable example of human ingenuity and enterprise. It is, after all, the tallest building in the world at the time of writing. Its supremacy will only be challenged by the upcoming Kingdom Tower in Jeddah, Saudi Arabia, on the banks of the Red Sea. For the record, Burj Khalifa stands 828 meters tall. The Kingdom Tower will breach a kilometer in height. However, the Burj Khalifa remains the world's tallest structure for the time being.

It was expected that my first stop in this desert outpost would be Burj Khalifa. The view from this sky-piercing complex was breathtaking. The scale is seen to be believed. You may have seen the movies from the Mission Impossible and Fast and Furious franchises, which have a few action sequences within this tower. However, even such larger-than-life films cannot appropriately capture the splendor of this larger-than-life tower. To add to the grandeur of the sight, the Burj Khalifa comes complete with several shopping complexes, mammoth aquariums, and unending indoor ski slopes. I was lucky to participate in the 'At the Top' event. Fortunately, the weather cooperated on that particular day. We were whisked away into a special lift, and the ascent began.

I have been in many elevators. I expected to reach the top in some time. However, when I looked at the display counter, the numbers were whizzing past. Before I knew it, I was on Floor 125. I stepped out on the deck for the 360-degree views. There were another 37 stories above me, and they seemed to go on. As I looked down the 456 meters to the earth, the surrounding towers appeared small in comparison. Then I saw the metropolis that stretched out before me. The vistas were breathtaking, and any first-time visitor should not miss out on this once-in-a-lifetime opportunity. I am not acrophobic, but I can get a bit squeamish at great heights. But not here. I was only left with sheer astonishment.

We stayed at The Palms, Atlantis. We had views of the tranquil blue seas of the Arabian Gulf and the spectacular Dubai cityscape as the resort is one of the crown jewels of Palm Jumeirah.

The Palm, Atalntis

The region, which is known for underwater hotel rooms and Dubai's largest waterpark, has lots of fun, cuisine, and family adventure to offer for day visitors and Atlantis guests. Aquaventure Waterpark promises a world of adventure that will make you feel different in the water in a variety of ways. The park has been featured on international television shows such as "The Amazing Race." Over 100 rides and watersports experiences are spread over three towers at this extreme theme park. The most memorable and my favorite of them is the record-breaking "Leap of Faith" at Neptune Tower. It is a freefall water slide, and if someone blindfolded you and took you to the slide entrance, you will not realize what you are about to do. The starting point is part of an alcove, and it is nondescript that it would seem innocuous. Then when you get on the slide, you will drop nearly 60 feet vertically (9 stories) down. If that is not thrilling enough, the slide passes through a terrifying shark tank!

The hotel also features a once-in-a-lifetime yoga session at the Lost Chambers Aquarium. Why is this experience unique? The setting is the sell here as you will think you have stumbled upon a fantastical as sunlight streams down the Atlantis-themed waters. Everything is covered, from the yoga mat to complimentary water, so that you can concentrate only on your technique. Even as you exert and contour your body into different positions, you will find your breath stable and relaxed as you look into the waters and see the fish calmly swim across the waters. You can even get up close and personal with the aquatic life of The Lost Chambers Aquarium by taking a twilight dive into their world after observing them during your yoga session. Fear not if you do not have any prior diving experience and expertise. They will equip you with the Aquatrek system, and the Aquatrek helmet provides far better sight than a regular diving mask. The best time to take a dive? Twilight. Many aquatic species become more active after dusk making for one of the best sights in the world. You will take in the experience lit up by the final rays of the sun and your portable lights.

The island also featured two of my favorite restaurants in Dubai. The first one served the traditional Middle Eastern cuisine in Ayamna. The restaurant offers lovely outdoor seating and the hummus is to die for! I loved the other delicacies on offer like the falafel. There was so much flavor and complexity in what can seem like a humble dish. However, there would be some element to elevate your senses. One such item was Mouhamara. It is an Arabic chili paste with spiced walnuts, pistachio, and chili oil. However, the highlight was the sawdust dejaj. It is a succulent chicken dish with a good amount of spice and is pan-fried. Each bite was absolutely tender and juicy.

The other restaurant was Street Pizza by Gordon Ramsay. I had seen the famous chef on many shows and I have associated him with his screams and rants. However, my experience at this restaurant gave me an entirely new perspective. You will be mistaken to think of this place as any regular old pizzeria. It featured unlimited pizza and coke. Just imagine it as a Michelin-starred pizza restaurant with no limits. It also pushed culinary explorations. One of the enduring associations of pizza is its cheese. However, we had a vegan pizza and it was amazing. In fact, I must admit that it was even better than the underwhelming Margherita that we had.

However, there is more to Dubai than just the glitz and glamor of a slick urban life. If I were to borrow the words of Sting from his song, *Desert Rose*, Dubai could be aptly summed as:

> *I dream of fire*
> *Those dreams are tied to a horse that will never tire*
> *And in the flames*
> *Her shadows play in the shape of man's desire*
> *This desert rose*
> *Each of her veils*
> *A secret promise*
> *This desert rose....*

Dubai, the city, is formed from the crucible of man's desire to reshape and rescale human civilization. However, the veils of Dubai can be found away from the urban lifestyle. Just 30-40 minutes away from the city limits are the desert landscapes civilization yet to trod. The desert safaris are breathtaking and gorgeous. Away from the thumping beats of clubs, traffic, and urban sprawl comes the tunes of wind as it whips up sand from the waves of dunes. The tranquility of the desert can take you by surprise. The sheer swathes of desert lands will finally leave you with an inkling of the majesty of nature. Humanity challenged it and put up a city called Dubai, and then you see the desert, and you will realize how the stunning simplicity of sand can conjure such magnificence. You can explore these fascinating sights via guided excursions or Dubai desert safaris. There are many options for the safaris. There are the sunset and sunrise safaris. You may associate sunrise and sunsets with the beaches and urban landscapes. You can see the sun setting or rising behind urban structures or over the ocean. But the desert? It is almost meditational in its experience. You can see an orange-tinted ball in a sepia-stained sky setting over and behind the ochre sand dunes.

Camel Rock, Red Dunes

Then there is the safari that lets you experience the traditional Arabic lifestyle and hospitality, where you are taken to a Bedouin-style campsite. I opted for the more fun and thrilling Dune Bash. An expert driver will take you on a pulse-racing adventure on the dunes on a powerful 4x4 vehicle. We were taken in a Land Rover. The sand that gets thrashed up as the vehicle drives through the dunes makes for one cinematic visual. Of course, this visual look stunning from outside the vehicle. It is quite different from the inside as you try to comprehend driving on extremely packed but loose sand and not on firm asphalt. However, the adrenaline rush from the ride will leave you breathless. A word of caution, do this on an empty stomach as you don't want to throw up inside the vehicle as sand is thrown up outside. We finished the safari by opting for the relatively gentler camel ride to a luxury campsite. The ride can be wobbly, but after the heavy exertions of the four-wheel drive, you will find the four-legged animal more comforting and cooler. There are other things to explore when on a desert safari. You can go quad biking and get your hands tattooed with traditional henna designs. If you wish to be a little more adventurous, you can try falconry. You will be treated to a lavish barbeque treat at the end of the day.

After the desert safari, we drove to Burj Al Arab (I have been told it can be accessed from 3 routes). This hotel is extravagance on steroids. If you want to feel like royalty in Dubai, go to Burj Al Arab. The Burj Al Arab is an iconic landmark representing wealth at its finest, opulent best. The blue water wall is an absolutely stunning sight. It translates to English as the Tower of the Arabs. It is a 7-star hotel and is one of the tallest hotels in the world. However, there are only 202 rooms available in the hotel. The low number of rooms can be attributed to the fact that 39 percent of its overall structure is non-occupiable. It is one of the iconic landmarks of the man-made islands of Dubai. The tower is on an island about 920 feet off Jumeriah Beach, managed by the Jumeirah Hotel Company, and linked to the mainland by a private, curved bridge. The hotel is instantly recognizable because the structure is built to imitate the sail of a ship.

The hotel features a helipad near the roof, 210 meters (689 feet) above ground. The hotel has an overall floor space of 117 meters (153 feet) by 33 meters (108 feet). The latter is a consequence of the hotel being built on an artificial island rather than a natural one, transmitted through a system of piers and cables. The tops of the posts are capped with wooden summits that provide more indoor space for meetings and events. These structures were designed with breeze towers meant to keep guests cool by exchanging air temperature with the surrounding environment. The project was awarded the Japan Gold prize in the international architecture competition in 2013. When I stood at its foot, I could not help but marvel at the flawless, gleaming glass that rose in front of me. I will always remember the taste of the 24-carat gold cappuccino served at Burj Al Arab. It was expensive but is once in lifetime indulgence. We were lucky to get a chance to look from the sky view bar, and what a view!

Dubai is the epitome of glamor and wealth. As I moved past those skyscrapers and the lavish Armani residencies, my mind took me back to the magazine pages when Dubai was not the city of wealth and gold. Today, the United Arab Emirates (or UAE's) economy is now the fifth-largest in the Middle East (after Turkey, Saudi Arabia, Egypt, and Iran), with a GDP of US$421 billion (AED 1.5 trillion) in 2020. But it is growing faster than most other Arab countries and is on track to become the third-largest economy in the world by the end of the decade. With oil prices dropping to US$26 a barrel in 2020, the country's finances are under even more pressure than they were in October 2014, when it announced its first budget. However, with oil prices on the rebound, there is an added buzz in the Middle East.

However, one can also see the a being made by Dubai. There has been a renewed focus on the tourism sector. It contributed to 4.6% of the GDP in 2017 or $41 billion in 2017. It created about 570,000 jobs (4.8% of the total jobs) in the city. In fact, the contribution of the tourism sector to the GDP rose by 138% in the ten years from 2007 to 2017.

But it is not as rosy as first pictured. The number of hotel rooms has grown seven-fold since 2007, going from 283,000 to 1.2 million. Yet average hotel room occupancy has dropped from 4.2 to 3.7 over the same period. However, the city might be seeing some change. In 2016, the Dubai International Airport (DXB) recorded a footfall of 83.6 million, and in the same year, 14.9 million guests patronized

Dubai hotels. This is an increase of 5% compared to the previous year.

The government could also be prepared to face the uncertainties of the global market. There can be no greater lesson than that of the crash of the global financial markets in 2008. The government's determination to shift from a trade-based yet oil-reliant economy to one centered on services and tourism led to a property bubble from 2004 to 2008. Large-scale construction has transformed Dubai into one of the world's fastest-growing cities.

As a tourist, the city has offered grandiose, which I am still carrying with me in the form of memories and photographs; amidst the pomp of the city, I recall the soothing Al Seef, a wonderful seaside resort brought to you by the Meraas. It is located near the famed district of Al Fahidi in Bur Dubai. This delightful site has a wonderful ambiance, and the banks of the river give respect to Emirati history. Many travelers come here for the café culture since many eateries have open-air seating. You may learn about Al Seef's modern take on local culture while taking in breathtaking views of the waterfront treasures and the Creek. The Dhows (traditional wooden boats), which are enchantingly lighted at night, add to the charm. They allow tourists to have a delectable supper on board while cruising the Creek's tranquil waters. Al Seef provides a flawlessly matched retail therapy experience, fusing current brands with classic elegance. You have the opportunity to sample and enjoy the finest of both the West and the East. Traditional handicrafts, meticulous craftsmanship, and local talent may be found alongside cutting-edge fashion names, providing you with a refuge of comfort, style, and luxury.

I will never forget the Wild Wadi waterpark. It has over 30 thrilling rides based on Arabian folktales, including the iconic character Juha. Every ride in the Wild Wadi waterpark is linked to a story about Juha's trip, which both children and adults enjoy. Flood River's meter-high waves, a trip through amazing Tantrum Alley, bodyboarding at Wipeout Flowrider, and relaxing in the Wave Pool are available to visitors. The Master Blaster attraction, a gravity-defying water roller-coaster, is another feature of the waterpark. Wild Wadi features a large assortment of water rides suitable for people of all ages. It is beautifully constructed with the highest levels of safety in mind.

Certain things stand out only in Dubai. Not just the extravagance but its people. Before I landed in Dubai, I did not know I could speak in my own mother tongue in a foreign land. Most of the taxi drivers speak Hindi. In the cab that took us to our hotel, I learned so much about him and his struggles. I will not deny it, but there is a distinct ecstasy when you speak your own language in a foreign place. I learned that in Dubai, most of the population is from India, Bangladesh, the Philippines, Sri Lanka, Nepal, and China. I was surprised to learn that Dubai is the shortest international distance via flight from Delhi after Nepal. We experienced various incidents, and now when I look back, I wonder whether it was a dream. Take, for instance, we wanted to take a taxi at Burj Al Arab, and an S class Mercedes rolled in! We were apprehensive and thought they would charge us astronomical rates. But to our surprise, they set the same as normal rates. Such an experience is only possible in Dubai. If you enjoy shopping, Dubai is a must-visit destination. The Dubai Outlet Malls are one place you will like. Over 100 large format retailers and brands are housed in these huge structures. The Dubai Mall and Mall of emirates are places to shop for brands you wish with the latest collection on offer. One needs to be clear on card spending limits as you are mesmerized by the range the place has to offer.

This city has many great spots with great delicacies to offer. My personal favorite remains the Cheesecake Factory in Dubai Mall. I always wanted to visit one, but we don't have a franchise in India yet. Thankfully, I was able to go to this outlet in Dubai. We had a tropical ginger cooler with stuffed mushrooms, loaded baked potato tots, and fried cheese. It was definitely high in calories, but they were so lip-smackingly delicious.

I also enjoyed the Beet and Avocado Salad, Crispy Brussel Sprouts (wonderfully cooked), and my beloved Korean Fried Cauliflower from various places in Dubai.

I loved the cafeteria-style restaurants. They are fun, easy to manage, and great for family dining. I had the opportunity to visit the authentic Emirati restaurant AL Jawareh, located in the heart of Dubai. Jumeriah and Ali Mohammed established the restaurant in 1972 when they were students in Dubai. Over the years, the restaurant has developed a reputation as a fine-dining spot serving traditional Emirati food.

If you want to experiment with Emirato cuisine, I highly recommend the Luqaimat. It is a popular Arabic delicacy crunchy on the surface and soft and fluffy on the inside. These honey-glazed doughnut balls are covered with sesame seeds. However, the sweet also has a Turkish equivalent called Lokma. Lokma is made by mixing ground nuts with *tvlok* (Arabic for wheat flour) and portrays the distinctive flavor of the Middle Eastern country.

I recall having Margoogat, a stew that blew my taste buds away with its massive meaty flavor cooked with garam masala spices and veggies. Margoogat can be made in various ways depending on the primary component, which might be chicken, lamb, or even potatoes. The meal is available at various restaurants in Dubai, ranging from small diners to the most expensive hotels. It's also a terrific Ramadan recipe to make at home. With garlic, turmeric, bezar, and cumin, this was one of the greatest stews I've ever eaten. I favored the lamb-based variety over the chicken-based one.

Through the boundaries of glitzy Dubai, I uncovered a rich history and cultural legacy that sparked from the Al Fahidi Quarter. It was replete with all of the previous Dubai's traditional touches. Dubai, I learned, distinguishes itself apart from the rest of the UAE's equivalents due to its large number of professionals and immigrants. More than 200 different nationalities are represented in the city, a figure that increases every year. With the largest concentration of foreigners living in the Al Fahidi area, I could sense that this was a place where different cultures would converge. As a foodie, I empathized with the traffic congestion and the overwhelming slog of centerless consumerism. I also understood the power of location choice in reaping the rewards.

The Al Fahidi area, after all, is where many of the city's most popular restaurants are located. Dubai is a once-in-a-lifetime opportunity, and I consider myself lucky enough to have visited this grand place. To suppose such a metropolis might be developed in the desert is, in my opinion, to envision a mirage. It truly is a city with it all: entertainment, business, culture, and so much more! Now when I am locked at home jotting this down almost having the second trip to Dubai, reliving those moments, I feel rejuvenated. Well, you can have one trip twice if you enjoy it enough first by visiting the place and second by relieving the place in your mind.

15

HONG KONG

"Remember, You're The One Who Can Fill The World With Sunshine."
— Snow White

Weren't we all fond of fairy tales? If not all of you can relate, I am sure some of you are like me, who remain amazed every time they read fairy tales. It was my dream to meet the Disney princesses in real life as a kid, and I always thought it was only a dream. How can I possibly meet Snow White, Sleeping Beauty, or Rapunzel? How can I ever shake my hands with Mickey Mouse or meet all my favorite characters?

I had so many questions prepared for them, about the evil stepmother, about the monsters. When I learned I was visiting Hong Kong, the eight-year-old me was too excited. Disney so enchanted me that as the plane was touching down, sI removed my seat belt to peep through the window. I wished they could just offer a special landing directly to Disney Land, and this giddy behavior of mine fetched me some glares from the cabin crew.

Instead of confessing my excitement, I simply asked for a glass of water to cover it up.

As soon as I landed in Hong Kong, I realized the city was a gigantic hub of grandeur and magnificence. The Hong Kong skyline is distinct and recognizable, with approximately 1500 buildings taller than 100 meters. It is a spectacular experience, with some of the world's highest skyscrapers and wonderful vantage spots to observe the skyline. Great cities have awe-inspiring skylines in common, and Hong Kong's skyline is one of the best, with the natural Victoria Peak and its spread of high rises. The skyline of this huge urban jungle is dominated by skyscrapers that have served as the background to some of the most exciting moments in blockbuster films. The skyline depicts the city's evolution over time and how well it mixes with its surroundings. Hong Kong has over 300 buildings over 150 meters tall and about 60 structures over 200 meters tall, making it one of the world's most densely populated cities. While it is breathtaking during the day, Hong Kong Skyline Night is an extraordinarily vivid sight at night, making it one of the city's main draws for visitors from all over the globe.

Hong Kong Skyline

Finally, the much-awaited moment came, and my dear readers, this was a dream come true moment. Disneyland in Hong Kong is a world full of enchantment, pleasure, laughter, and adventure. Disneyland, which has enchanted visitors from all over the world, is the only location where one's fantasy may come to life. And in order for you to fully appreciate this paradise, here is a custom-made guide that will lead you to have unlimited fun with your family and friends on your next vacation to Hong Kong.

Disneyland in Hong Kong, located in the middle of Lantau Island, is Asia's second-largest Disneyland. It is heavily influenced by Chinese culture, customs, and traditions, and visiting such a marvel is one of the top things to do in Hong Kong.

Hong Kong Disneyland

The fantastic voyage begins on Main Street, United States of America. It spans Hong Kong Disneyland's main gate to the Sleeping Beauty Castle. Main Street USA's buildings and layouts are nearly identical to those at Disneyland Anaheim, and the entire décor is built primarily of wood.

It depicts a little village in late-nineteenth-century and early-twentieth-century America. It is home to the Animation Academy, City Hall, Town Square, and the Emporium, the greatest souvenir shop in the city. This is also the best spot to watch the spectacular fireworks display. You may also visit the Bibbidi Bobbidi Boutique or the Royal Princess Garden, where children can dress up as their favorite princess or prince. At the Market House Bakery or the Plaza Inn, you may sample some of the world's greatest desserts. You may take a break at the Corner café in the afternoon.

Disneyland is the happiest place on earth, and it certainly is more than just a marketing spin. Seeing Sleeping Beauty's Castle, witnessing a parade, or riding the It's a Small World attraction has a certain allure. Its allure is difficult to resist. My experience in Disneyland not only quenched my childhood desire to meet the princesses but also allowed me to meet my favorite Star Wars heroes. The 'Fairy Tale Forest' charmingly recreates fairytales, the 'Sword in the Stone Show' challenges visitors to recover the mythical sword Excalibur from a massive stone to show their worthiness.

Despite its tiny size compared to other theme parks, Toy Story Land is the first of the theme parks to open since Hong Kong Disneyland's founding. Woody and his buddies will meet you with a warm welcome against a backdrop of large blades of bamboo grass and featured toys, soldiers, and alphanumeric blocks distributed around Andy's courtyard's toy-box area.

RC Racer is a thrilling thrill trip set on a 27-meter race track that will keep your adrenaline pumping as you sit in a cute automobile. I enjoyed the Toy Soldier Parachute Drop, which takes you to the top of a large tower before plunging down and up while you take in the sights and enjoy this fantastic ride with your family. The Slinky Dog Spin is an exciting ride on an adorable caterpillar-styled pleasure ride. At the same time, the Barrel of Fun lets you snap photographs with iconic Toy-Story characters such as Woody, Jessie, and their gang. The Toy Soldier Boot Camp is also shown, where toy soldiers will be taught combat roles in fights. We stayed in the hotel Disney land; I had great fun getting lost and playing in the maze.

Hotel Disney

We had an amazing dinner experience which fulfilled my desire to meet Mickey and other characters and Belle. I could also meet and greet with the other Disney princesses like Snow White, Cinderella, Ariel, Jasmine, among others. We went around Christmas, and the artificial snowfall mesmerized us along with Christmas songs.

Another most fascinating experience I have felt was at Ocean Park. We purchased our tickets at the counters and immediately began exploring the attractions at Ocean Park Hong Kong. We began our excursion in Ocean Park, Hong Kong's upland area. We rode one of their larger roller coasters (there are two). Because it was built on elevated terrain, it wasn't so much of a thriller. You should not miss their "The Abyss" ride; it was an incredible adrenaline rush! The rollercoaster essentially lifted us 185 feet into the air before dropping us in free fall for 5 seconds. Ocean Park Hong Kong's four-story aquarium (dubbed Atoll Reef) is also not to be missed, since it is one of the park's most popular attractions. It's something I've seen a lot of images of and have always wanted to see for myself. Of all the breathtaking experiences so far, the one which still makes me smile and I re-live it every now and then by probing back to these days is my encounter with cute pandas. The charming Giant Pandas, who are a draw for tourists and a must-see, especially if you have never seen these rare and endangered species before, are one of Ocean Park's cherished inhabitants. I can't believe I've met the Giant Panda! We were taken to see and use the facilities by the animal keepers, and we even got to meet and feed the giant panda!

Looking at this city glittered with lights and joy, and after experiencing these out-of-the-world sensations, I wondered about its history. After researching the place, I found out today's Hong Kong has been a site of human habitation since the Old Stone Age. It became a part of the Chinese empire with its loose integration into the Qin dynasty (221–206 BC). It began as an agricultural fishing community and a salt production site before evolving into a major free port and a significant international financial center.

The Treaty of Nanjing, which ended the First Opium War, saw the Qing dynasty cede Hong Kong to the British Empire in 1842. The British also triumphed in the Second Opium War, compelling the Qing Empire to relinquish Kowloon in 1860 and lease the New Territories for 99 years beginning in 1898.

During World War II, Japan controlled Hong Kong from 1941 until 1945. Hong Kong was freed by a joint British-Chinese force and reverted to British control after the war in 1945. During the Korean War and the Great Leap Forward, Hong Kong's population grew dramatically due to migrants from mainland China. Hong Kong evolved from the jurisdiction of entrepôt trade to one of industry and manufacture in the 1950s. Manufacturers were compelled to migrate to the mainland due to China's economic reforms, prompting Hong Kong to strengthen its commercial and financial sectors.

Hong Kong should draw confidence from its long-term evolution and resistance to unfavorable circumstances over the previous half-century as it enters a new era of growth with the return to Chinese sovereignty. For a long time, economists have been fascinated by Hong Kong's ability to thrive in the face of change.

A groundbreaking assessment of Hong Kong's economic growth was published over 40 years ago. Hong Kong's economy was in shambles when it was released on August 30, 1945, following four years of captivity. After ten years, the Colony was known as one of the most affluent colonies in the Far East. It's tough to come up with a comparable example of economic development. The first thing that comes to me is how to describe this unique economic growth story.

However, as intriguing as the progress achieved during the 1950s may have looked, it pales in contrast to what has been accomplished in succeeding decades, particularly after the 1970s. Hong Kong was part of a radically different world in 1997. It has evolved into one of the world's most important trade, business, and financial hubs. Hong Kong has grown into an economic powerhouse, with GDP equivalent to US$155 billion, total trade worth over US$440 billion, and bank assets valued at over one trillion US dollars in 1996, despite its small population (about 6.4 million people, slightly smaller than Switzerland) and area (1,095 square kilometers, about a third larger than New York City). With its integration into the global service economy, Hong Kong had grown to become the world's seventh-largest trading entity and the stock market, the world's fifth-largest banking center in terms of external financial transactions, and the world's fifth-largest foreign exchange market in terms of average daily turnover, the world's fourth-largest source of foreign direct investment, the world's busiest container port, and one of the world's most prosperous economies, with per capita GDP of US$7,500 in 1996.

Today, these buildings that add grandeur to the city are the powerhouses of its economy. The International Commerce Centre (ICC), which stands at 484 meters, is a record-breaking skyscraper and a significant tourist attraction in Hong Kong. Because it is the highest structure, it can take everything to new heights! The International Commerce Centre has the world's tallest hotel, the world's highest swimming pool, and Hong Kong's highest observation deck.

The top 16 levels of the structure are occupied by the Ritz Carlton hotel, which occupies most of the skyscraper's 118 floors. The structure contains several tourist attractions that will keep all tourists enthralled throughout the day. The HSBC Tower is a well-known edifice in the city. With a price tag of $650 million, it was the most expensive building in the world when it was completed in 1986 by famous architect Norman Foster. In fact, it was this building that made Norman Foster a global phenomenon. Foster would go on to become closely associated with pioneering high-tech architecture and British modernist architecture. The HSBC Tower comprises just 52 stories, but it was the first of its kind to be constructed entirely of structural steel, with no reinforced concrete in the core. The building was constructed in modular portions elsewhere and connected on the spot because of the city's restrictions on nighttime construction and the project's urgency. Even though the public observation deck on the 43rd level has been closed to visitors since 2014, travelers still flock to the structure for its unusual architecture. The triangular framework, which is brilliantly illuminated, is meant to resist earthquakes while still being visually appealing. It's awe-inspiring to view the city's highest buildings all close together during tourist trips.

The four key industries in the Hong Kong economy include financial services, trading and logistics, tourism, and producer and professional services. They have been the engine of Hong Kong's economic growth, spurring the expansion of other industries and creating jobs.

Studying the economic growth of Hong Kong and witnessing the development left me stunned. At that point in time, I perhaps have traveled as a traveler quenching her dreamy desires of Disney world and experiencing the city life of Hong Kong. Now, as a commerce student when I am looking back and studying the growth the realization of Hong Kong is hitting me on a different level.

Amidst all the luxuries the city had to offer, satisfying culinary expectations was another surprise the city had to offer. Due to Hong Kong's past as a British colony and its long history as an international port of commerce, there are multiple influences.

European cuisines (especially British cuisine), Cantonese cuisine, and non-Cantonese Chinese cuisines, chiefly Teochew, Shanghainese, Hokkien, and Hakka, dominate. Hong Kong has been dubbed "Gourmet Paradise" and "World's Fair of Food" due to its complex combinations and worldwide gourmet competence.

It is not just the lavish hotels that serve up delicious food. There are food kiosks on the street. They are generally run by one or two persons driving a cart. The carts allow the chef to offer refreshments in whichever location is most crowded at any given time. Tight health laws and various types of lease vs. licensed hawker limitations have put a strain on this mobile food culture, which was prominent in the 1970s and 1980s. Cantonese food is the backbone of Hong Kong's home-cooking and dining scenes, as it is the most prominent cultural group in the city. Many early well-known Cantonese restaurants, such as Tai San Yuan and Luk Yu Tea House, were Hong Kong outposts of famous Guangzhou restaurants. Until the 1970s, most chefs in Hong Kong were trained in the Guangzhou restaurant sector. The majority of Hong Kong's well-known cuisine came from Guangzhou and was typically developed with an awareness of international preferences. Cantonese cuisine costs are likely to be the most diverse, ranging from the cheapest lou mei to the extremely expensive abalone specialties.

I tried the famous cart noodle. It is a noodle dish, as its name suggests, that gained popularity in Hong Kong and Macau in the 1950s thanks to independent street sellers who used carts to sell noodles on roadsides and in public housing estates in low-income areas. Many street sellers have departed, but the noodle's name and look have become cultural icons. We also tried meat grilled on spits over an open fire or in a huge wood-burning rotisserie oven, known as siu mei in Cantonese. It produces a distinct, rich barbecue taste, and the roast is frequently covered with a tasty sauce before roasting (a different sauce is used for each type of meat). Siu mei is particularly popular among Cantonese emigrants in Hong Kong and Macau and Chinatowns abroad. Steamed meatballs are a popular dim sum dish in Cantonese cuisine.

It's popular in Hong Kong and other Chinatowns throughout the world. Meatballs are often cooked with minced meat, water chestnut for texture, coriander, and a few slivers of Cheung pei or dried orange peel for spice. To keep the meatballs from resting in the cooking liquids, a layer of tofu skin or peas is added to lift them from the bottom of the dish. It's usually accompanied by Worcestershire sauce. This kind of cuisine includes dishes derived from Western global cuisines but is not defined by nation.

Outside of Hong Kong, it's known as Canto-Western food or Hong Kong-style Western cuisine. Restaurants that cater to travelers would certainly have both east and west menus. Most foods include Chinese and Cantonese characteristics, such as meat marinated in soy sauce, served in a soy sauce-dominated gravy with fried rice on the side, or pasta. Fresh seafood meals dominate the menus of Hong Kong restaurants and marketplaces, including entire steamed fish sold at Sai Kung Street market. I tried fried rice, black bean with scallops, and noodles but subsequently learned from the hotelier that the ideal way to start was with steamed fish and Lamma. Another local delicacy was stinky tofu, which was considered one of Hong Kong's strangest dishes owing to the fermented tofu's strong odor. My favorite dining establishment was the Kau Kee Food Café, located on Gough Street in Central Hong Kong. I couldn't stop trying everything, from the silky-smooth wheat noodles to the thick broth. Hong Kong expertly combined fun, adventure, sightseeing, and culture to provide us with a vacation that would live long in our memories.

When I look back at my days in Hong Kong, the skyline, the fascinating Victoria Peak, the Aberdeen Fishing Village, and a cool Harbour Cruise are among the city tour highlights. With the amazing "Symphony of Lights," a music and light performance, and the extraordinary world of magic, The Disney Land, I realize that I have never bid adieu to this city. I am carrying Hong Kong in my heart and soul, and I visit this place every time I close my eyes.

16

SINGAPORE

"I can't believe this airport has a butterfly garden and a movie theater. JFK is just salmonella and despair."
— Rachel Chu

Neither could I believe I was here, in the same city where one of my favorite movies Crazy Rich Asians, was shot. As soon as I landed at the same airport, I felt like part of a movie. The aura of the place was surreal. Believe me, when I say that I have visited so many wonderful cities all, but Singapore has the best airport. It is almost like another city in a town, an epitome of technological advancement at the display. There's a lot more for nature lovers to see and do here! Feed the fish at the Koi Pond every day at 9 a.m. and 4 p.m. Stroll around the Sculptural Tree Garden's high walkways and get close to the greenery on the tree-like sculptures. In the Water Lily Garden, marvel at the colorful aquatic plants such as the Sacred Lotus and Amazon Water Lily. Changi Airport's ten gardens have intriguing mysteries just waiting to be uncovered. It's no surprise that Changi Airport is routinely listed among the world's top airports, with so many natural experiences to discover — all for free.

Singapore is one of the greenest cities on the planet. This skyscraper-filled metropolis is also surrounded by lush nature. Green cover covers about half of Singapore's geographical area (roughly 700 square kilometers). Pockets of new plant life are located in the oddest settings, beyond the various parks and gardens.

My experience in this wonderful city is special. It is something extraordinary. Singapore is regarded as a joyful location for all travelers, be it, adults or children as there are several experiences in this interesting country. This town has a lot of fascinating things to do, especially for folks visiting with their families. It boasts of having Universal Studios, the rainforest zoo, and the SEA aquarium in its wardrobe. It is said when a prince from Sumatra came to the island and spotted an auspicious lion, he is said to have created Singapore. He constructed a city there and named it Singapura, which means 'the lion city,' believing it to be a good omen. The "Lion City," as it is referred to, has a beautiful blend of Malaysian, Chinese, Indian, Arab, and English cultures – all with their very own Singapore twists. Singapore is presently a modern, industrialized society, with entrepôt trade continuing to play a vital role in its economy, thanks to the considerable groundwork laid by the country's founding fathers. Singapore has surpassed Hong Kong and Rotterdam as the busiest transshipment port. I was so excited from the day the planning of the trip began. I was really sad when my father said he wouldn't be able to accompany my grandparents, my mother and me. As soon as we landed, breathing the Singapore air, I felt elevated. Our B&B was situated amid Orchard Street, next to the Shangri-La Hotel, giving us easy access to Singapore's Metro, one of the greatest globally.

We first went to Gardens by the Bay. We were able to learn about several sorts of plants kept in giant seashell-shaped greenhouses that simulated icy mountain temperatures while traveling with my mother, a plant enthusiast. It's a location where marvels blossom into stunning works of art. The nation's aim to turn the entire "City into a Garden" included Gardens by the Bay. It is on the list of Singapore's must-see sights.

The Gardens by the Bay are separated into three sections: Bay Central Garden, Bay East Garden, and Bay South Garden, and are located on the Marina Bay coastline. It is, without a doubt, one of the most surreal locations on Earth. Gardens by the Bay is surrounded by lush green beauty over 101 hectares and holds over 21,000 plants from over 800 distinct kinds. It's one of the few places where nature and technology coexist, resulting in a real-world treasure.

The garden is even more spectacular at night when the entire park shines with lights created by solar energy stored throughout the day. It's a fantastic spot to be with your loved ones because of the lovely perfume of exotic flowers and the magnificent lighting. The Cloud Forest is a visual treat for the eyes, with a cool interior and a 35-foot waterfall surrounded by green walls and orchids. It mimics the tropical environment of South East Asia and Middle East Asia across an area of 0.8 hectares inside the South Bay. The floral dome was crowned the world's largest greenhouse by the Guinness Book of Records in 2015. Exotic blooms from several continents are displayed in the dome.

The Supertrees are 16-story man-made trees with gorgeous vines and ferns. The OCBC Skyway is an elevated bridge that winds around the supertrees and allows you to stroll over them and a better look at the exotic ferns. We also walked the spectacular 128-meter-long skywalk and had the opportunity to attend the Light and Sound performance. This place is embedded in my heart forever, as my beloved grandparents had bought me a beautiful floral necklace with my initials on it, my most prized possession. Every time I wear it, I can see this place with my eyes closed.

The next day brought me another bundle of joy as my father surprised us by joining the trip. We went to visit Sentosa Island. Sentosa Island is Singapore's top entertainment destination, with a complex of museums, thrilling amusement parks, theatres, world-class 5-star hotels, golf courses, and pure white sand beaches throughout the island. Sentosa is a recreational island off Singapore's southern shore. Road, cable car, pedestrian boardwalk, and monorail link it to the Singapore mainland. Sentosa is home to a variety of attractions for visitors of all ages, including world-class resorts, Michelin-starred restaurants, shopping, theme parks, the SEA Aquarium, the Tiger Sky Tower, adventure activities, and beaches (manmade beaches, can you believe it?). Although there are other ways to get to Sentosa, the Cable car is the best option if you want to make your journey truly unforgettable. The greatest panoramic view of the port and island may be seen here. It's weird, but also a little frightening. It was really funny to see my grandparents' reactions. It was their first time on a cable car and I made sure to capture their reactions to relish the moment forever. Now sitting back at home when I watch their jolly faces with a massive tinge of fear and excitement my heart gets so full. We were enticed to go about and explore Sentosa from the time we arrived. The first place we started with is Madame Tussauds.

Madame Tussauds in Singapore is the sixth branch of Asia's famed wax museum, and it embraces the elegance of Sentosa Island. Madame Tussauds Museum, which attracts a large number of international visitors each year, allows you to spend as much time as you like with your favorite celebrities.

The museum's main feature is a collection of realistic wax sculptures. Madame Tussauds offers it all, from wax sculptures of sports stars to sportsmen and historians. Visitors to this museum never fail to take a photo with their favorite celebrity's wax statue. For all of its visitors, Madame Tussauds Singapore is a wonderful combination of both magnificence and flair. Hold your breath if you believe that lifelike celebrity sculpture is all that Madame Tussauds Singapore has in store for you. The abundance of exciting things to do in Singapore will undoubtedly keep you amused from all angles.

I was able to take a photo with Taylor Swift, one of my favorite singers! My grandpa also had the opportunity to take a photo with the statue of our Prime Minister, Narendra Modi, whose mystique fascinates him. After that, my mother and grandparents visited the butterfly park. If it has not been clear, I despise insects to the depth of my being. Due to this phobia, I couldn't visit the park nonetheless, my beloved father kept me company and we had some delicious ice cream instead.

Grandparents at Sentosa

We got to the S.E.A Aquarium after a long trek. We were met with a massive glass wall with various aquatic animals moving in a beat as soon as we passed through the first tunnel. It was an unforgettable experience for us, especially because it was our first visit to a huge aquarium. We were all ecstatic to be able to see marine life up close, particularly large sharks and stingrays moving freely in the blue ocean. We felt as though we were going through the water. The SEA Aquarium is one of Asia's largest, featuring a wide range of marine animals. It was both exhilarating and calming at the same time. The simple act of sitting and watching these animals move was calming and relaxing.

Sentosa boasts a wide range of eateries that serve wonderful food. From quick food places to Michelin-starred eateries, there's something for everyone. Santosa Beaches are not only distinctive features that make it an ideal fun location, but the existence of extensive Sandy stretches adds to its allure.

Resort World, Sentosa

Sentosa boasts three man-made beaches that are bustling with activity. Siloso Beach is one of the most popular and often frequented beaches due to its proximity to public transportation.

The second Sentosa beach, Palawan, can be found walking west of Siloso. It's a long, broad beach that is perfect for families with kids. It has a suspension bridge that allows tourists to traverse what is considered to be Continental Asia's southernmost point. Tanjong Beach is Sentosa's quietest beach, owing to its distance from the 'Beach Station.' This beach is tranquil. The Wings of Time display is a must-see on our journey to Sentosa Island. The ultimate fusion of laser lights and sounds precisely coordinated with the movement of water, this multi-sensory outdoor display is the greatest fusion of laser lights and sounds. The finale of this stunning spectacle includes fireworks, which elevate the entire experience to a new level.

Our next day's destination was to visit the most popular Merlion. The Merlion can be seen at One Fullerton, in the Central Business District, and overlooking Marina Bay, at Merlion Park. The Merlion is positioned right close to the Fullerton Hotel for travelers who want to see it. Ask any friendly folks in the area where the Merlion is located, and they will gladly lead you there.

The Merlion

The Merlion monument, which towers majestically over Marina

Bay and spouts water into the Marina Basin 24 hours a day, 7 days a week, is a sight to behold. The Merlion transforms into a kaleidoscope of colors at night. As a tourist, I went to see the city's national symbol, the mythological Merlion, which has the body of a fish and the head of a lion. The Merlion Park monument, which sits near the mouth of the Singapore River, is one of the most recognized renditions of this iconic emblem. The Merlion's dual nature as a lion and a fish is a story that goes beyond the surface (or stone). The Merlion's fish-like body represents Singapore's beginnings as a fishing community known as Temasek—a name derived from the same root as tasek (Malay for "lake").

The head of the monument depicts Singapura, the city's original name (lion city in Sanskrit). Sang Nila Utama, a Srivijayan prince from Palembang, arrived on a beach after a storm at sea, according to folklore. The prince observed a strange beast at the Singapore River's entry, which he identified as a lion, and so Singapura was born. The Merlion statue stands 8.6 meters tall and weighs 70 tons, and it spits water from its mouth. It was created by local artist Lim Nang Seng and designed by Kwan Sai Kheong, and it was unveiled on September 15, 1972, near the mouth of the Singapore River by then-Prime Minister Lee Kuan Yew.

We went to Universal Studios the next day, and my favorite rides were Transformers, Puss in Boots, and The Dinosaur Ride. I also enjoyed viewing the Egyptian section of the park since I was fascinated with mythology (Percy Jackson and the Kane Chronicles for reference).

We also went to the aquarium, which is one of my mother's favorite places, and ate spaghetti at Boat Quay. Night Safari and Jurong Bird Park were two other sites we visited (the birds were magnificent). We also visited big retail malls such as Takashimaya. That's where I got my Mickey Mouse sneakers. Just outside Takashimaya, we enjoyed a fantastic falafel wrap. With the freshest falafel (chickpea) patties, the wrap contained some of the greatest hummus, labneh, and tabbouleh. We also ate at Clark Quay, where I had the finest tacos I'd ever tasted. The taco business was run by

Mexicans and offered delicious Birria Tacos (goat meat tacos). The tortillas are dipped in the thin layer of fat that floats to the top of the birria before being filled with meat and put on the griddle, which gives them their addictively crunchy texture. Birria tacos are topped with onions and cilantro and served with the consommé, or stew broth, on the side. The tacos are dipped in the consommé, which is made from the kisses of the cooks. We also had delicious tinga, which are chicken tacos, and my father had a flavorful burrito wrap with fajitas and pinto beans.

Without a doubt, the high-tech Lion city attracts a large number of visitors from all over the world. It is well-known for its captivating amusement park, renovated retail sector, and, of course, the magnificent urbane topography. One unforgettable in Singapore is the Singapore Zoo. On the one side, you have Singapore's numerous glamour and glam features, and on the other, you have its zoo. Singapore is a treasure trove with a globally famous zoo if you wish to wander your mind to its natural reserves.

The Singapore Zoo, the Night Safari, the Jurong Bird Park, and the River Safari are the four wildlife reserves in the city-state. The Singapore Zoo, which is just 40 years old, receives the most visitors each year, with 1.7 million, followed by the Night Safari with 1.1 million, and the Jurong Bird Park with 80,000. Though walking around the zoo is the best way to see it, the 28-hectare expanse is much too large to be explored altogether on foot. There are several rides available, including trams, boats, pony rides, and even horse carriages, which provide guests with a comprehensive experience. Rentable strollers are also offered for toddlers. Singapore Zoo is home to 300 species of animals, reptiles, and birds, and is spread out over a twenty-eight-hectare area. It is divided into 11 zones, each of which leads to a separate exhibit. The animals are housed in large, enclosed environments separated from visitors by moats filled with water or vegetation. Animals that may be dangerous to tourists are kept behind glass. The animals are given as much of a natural environment as possible, with just the most basic and necessary barriers erected to maintain a safe distance between people and the animals. To conserve the natural ecosystem, the majority of the land, as well as the water body, has been left alone. The Singapore Zoo has a total of 2800 animals on display. The zoo's enormous size, in terms of its animal reserve, makes it nearly difficult to see everything in a single visit. The finest aspect is that it raises them in an entirely natural environment.

Carnivores such as the white tiger, African Lion, leopards, cheetah, and wolverine, among others, call the wildlife reserve home. Siamang, orangutans, Rothschild giraffes, white rhinoceros, banded mongoose, Meerkat, Asian elephant, chimpanzee, Colobus monkey, Patas monkey, Capuchin monkey, Proboscis monkey, Hamadryas baboon, Sun bear, Arapaima, Mouse-deer, Indian star tortoise, and Komodo dragon are among the other species.

The reticulated python, Burmese python, Western diamondback rattlesnake, King cobra, Rhinoceros iguana, green iguana, python, chameleon, and Northern caiman lizard are among the reptiles found in the reptile reserve. The zoo in Singapore has an almost incomprehensible variety of creatures that will keep you intrigued for the whole day.

The Jungle Breakfast, which is the most thrilling and enjoyable manner of engaging with the animals, is one of my most unforgettable experiences. The orangutans and giraffes could see me up close and personal. Token feeding is permitted, which is thrilling for both adults and children. It was a really wonderful memory to be kept for a lifetime, especially with the keepers' constant commentary.

It is to be noted that Singaporean food, like its people, is ethnically diverse, integrating Malay, Chinese, Indonesian, Indian, and Western influences. A trip to one of the hawker centres or shopping mall food courts will be both educational and delicious.

From lowly street food carts to luxurious rooftop restaurants and everything in between, Singapore is foodie heaven. The Hainanese chicken rice was one of the dishes we tasted. It is rice cooked in chicken broth served with steamed chicken. This classic recipe is perfect for a fast and substantial lunch. The steamed rice bursting with flavor and a fragrant perfume is a testament to the high quality of the chicken stock used in this meal. Toss the chicken with some dipping sauce and try it. We also sampled some delectable chilli crabs. They were hard-shell crabs cooked in a tomato-chili-based semi-thick sauce. The partially cracked steamed crabs were briefly stir-fried in a mixture made of chilli sauce, ketchup, and eggs. Chilli crab, despite its name, is not particularly hot. To mop up the gravy, bread can be requested. So dive in with both hands! And there's the wonderful Laska, which combines Chinese and Malay cuisine by serving rice noodles in a spicy coconut curry soup with shrimp, fish cakes, egg, and chicken flesh. There are several other types of laksa, but the one popular in Singapore is katong laksa, which uses cut-up noodles. One must definitely visit Singapore, because apart from its rich history, the place is one of the most culturally and religiously diverse countries in the world, setting it apart from its neighbors.

The island has four official languages: English, Tamil, Malay, and Mandarin, and it observes many different religious holidays. Visitors may partake in gastronomic delights from many nations as well as see a variety of religious sites. Another compelling incentive to visit Singapore is that it is one of the world's cleanest cities. Singapore is free of foul odors and unattractive trash thanks to spitting and littering laws. Though some may criticize Singapore for being clinical, we believe that its immaculate streets are a major positive. Hundreds of hawker centers dot Singapore, where you can have a tasty dinner for around $10. A hawker center is comparable to a food court in a shopping mall, except that most of them are much larger. Hawker centers such as Newton Food Circus and Maxwell Hawker Centre have hundreds of items on sale, ranging from fresh seafood to laksa, as well as fresh fruit and local sweets.

Singapore, despite its tiny size, boasts a diverse range of restaurants serving cuisines from across the world at various pricing ranges. The Michelin guide is an excellent place to start if you're having trouble deciding amongst the apparently limitless selections of eateries. In recent years, there has been a significant increase in the number of local chefs crafting modern Singaporean cuisine. It's hard to think a street that used to be bordered by orchards is now full of shops where you want to shop till you drop. You may stroll the stores and shop for various designer items since there are approximately two dozen malls lining the two kilometers between Orchard MRT and Somerset MRT. The malls are also connected by an underground tunnel network to combat any bad weather conditions.

This journey provided us with some insights into Singapore, a country in my country's neighborhood. Everywhere I went, I took a lot of images. It is beneficial to young individuals like me who desire to travel throughout the world and learn more about other cultures

My curious mind as a student of economics once again compelled me to look at the economy of the city, I found that the most practical answer to Singapore's economic and employment problems was to embark on a thorough industrialization program, focusing on labor-intensive sectors. Regrettably, Singapore lacked an industrial history. The majority of its workforce was employed in commerce and services. As a result, they lacked competence and flexible abilities. Furthermore, without a hinterland and trading partners, Singapore was compelled to explore possibilities well outside its limits to propel its industrial growth.

In order to provide jobs for their citizens, Singapore's government began to experiment with globalization.

Singapore needed to develop a safe, corruption-free, and low-tax environment in order to attract investors. To make this possible, inhabitants of the country had to give up a significant amount of their liberty in exchange for a more authoritarian administration. International investors were attracted to the country's harsh yet business-friendly policies. Singapore was highly stable in comparison to its neighbors, who had volatile political and economic climates. Singapore, on the other hand, was a relatively stable place. Singapore was also a great spot to produce products because of its convenient location and well-developed port system.

In addition to its infrastructure, Singapore began to focus on improving its people resources. Many technical colleges were established, and foreign firms were paid to teach their unskilled personnel in computer technology, petrochemicals, and electronics. Those who were unable to find work in the industrial sector were placed in labor-intensive non-tradable services such as tourism and transportation.

Singapore is presently a modern, industrialized society, with entrepôt trade continuing to play a vital role in its economy, thanks to the considerable groundwork laid by the country's founding fathers. Singapore has surpassed Hong Kong and Rotterdam as the world's busiest transshipment port.

This is a journey I will cherish for the rest of my life, in this journey I have witnessed so many beautiful things, including the cheerful faces of my grandparents. I keep on thinking about the wonderful experiences we have had. Looking back at those days while being locked up at home brings solace to my mind.

CONCLUSION

> "What is this life if, full of care,
> We have no time to stand and stare.
> No time to stand beneath the boughs
> And stare as long as sheep or cows.
> No time to see, when woods we pass,
> Where squirrels hide their nuts in grass.
> No time to see, in broad daylight,
> Streams full of stars, like skies at night.
> No time to turn at Beauty's glance,
> And watch her feet, how they can dance.
> No time to wait till her mouth can
> Enrich that smile, her eyes began.
> A poor life this if, full of care,
> We have no time to stand and stare."
> — William Henry Davies

As I write this, the world is slowly opening again. My feet itch again to tread new ground and learn more new things. I encourage you, reader, to quickly spot your travel shoe and set off to collect the pebbles of memory and experience. People have many reasons to travel the world. For some, it is a way to see new cultures and expand their horizons. For others, it is a way to escape the everyday exertion and glimpse new and exciting places. Whatever the reason, there is no doubt that travel can be a rewarding experience. It could be any travel. It could be a traditional vacation with the family to a famous tourist spot. It could be an adventurous trip.

No matter how you choose to travel the world, do travel. It will always be a memorable experience. As I have explored in the pages before, you will see new cultures and learn about new people. Travel has a therapeutic impact. For me, it has been a way to connect with the world deeper, see the beauty in other cultures, and understand how cultures influenced the cuisines and how economies develop. It has also been my way to bond with family and friends, to create memories that will last a lifetime. I have found that the world has something to offer everyone.

Perhaps it was the lockdown. As I sat writing and reminiscing about these places, I got the leisure to reflect on my travels. I realise that I am lucky to have had the chance to broaden my horizons, and they made me all the better. There are many ways to measure oneself. For people of my age, it can be a variety of things. For some, it could be academic achievements. For others, it could be through their extra-curricular attainments. I can say with some pride that I do not fall behind in either category. However, I found accurate measures in my travels. It has shown me who I am, what I am capable of, and where I want to be. It has taught me lessons I could never have learned at home and has shown me sides of myself that I never knew existed.

Whenever I described my travels to my friends, I always did it from the perspective of showing the world I had seen. I am thankful that my father encouraged me to write this book as it has shown me. I love my picture taken at the famous tourist spots. Who doesn't? However, as you have read my book, you have also realized that my travels and sights have included my footpaths away from such spots. It is not the beaten path; it is my path. It is my path where I satisfy my curiosity about commerce, culture, and cuisine. It is a path where I have challenged myself to step outside of my comfort zone. It could be as simple as eating octopus in Greece or taking in stellar views atop tall buildings. I experienced new things. As I wrote this book, I realized that these experiences have been essential for my personal growth. I am constantly learning about different cultures and customs, which has taught me to be more tolerant and understanding of others. I have also gained a greater appreciation for my own culture and lifestyle. My travels have also helped me to develop independence and confidence. I have learned to rely on myself and to trust my instincts. I experienced that first-hand when I traveled to Germany for the second time without my parents. I was confident in taking my steps. I was open to new experiences, and each of these experiences has taught me new perspectives.

Today, I have found myself anew and more curious. At the beginning of the book, I talked about how I looked out the window and felt imprisoned. Now, when I look out the window, I find myself beckoned. There are many new miles to travel, new places to discover, cultures to rediscover, and cuisines to explore. Even the places I have revisited in this book call out to me, and I will go to them all to connect with them more profoundly. I want to find my memories in the nooks of these places and the stories and cuisines I missed. This is about the miles and moments gone and the miles and moments to come. As Mr Robert Frost rightly stated, "*And miles to go before I sleep. And miles to go before I sleep.*"

Thank You.

ABOUT THE AUTHOR

Manya Bhatia, budding economist; cuisine evangelist; social equality crusader, and global traveler is a 17-year-old student from India.

She has traveled to over 20 countries and over 35 international cities; has a deep interest in cuisines and what goes inside them; both as a food connoisseur and a promising chef.

Manya has a deep interest in public policy, marketing of brands, and the economics of the business and likes to connect the dots between history and its impact on culture, cuisine, and commerce.

She has done her summer school at the prestigious Harvard University.

Manya is Editor in Chief of Global Times; her school magazine and holds a leadership position on the school economic forum.

She expresses her thoughts through her blog - Mile Moments & Me. In her free time, she also paints and has a painting exhibit – Xpressions of an Indian Women as an ode to working women of India.

She has been actively involved with adult women through a help group where she has contributed to identifying needs for their education.

www.ingramcontent.com/pod-product-compliance
Lightning Source LLC
Chambersburg PA
CBHW032356040426
42451CB00006B/33